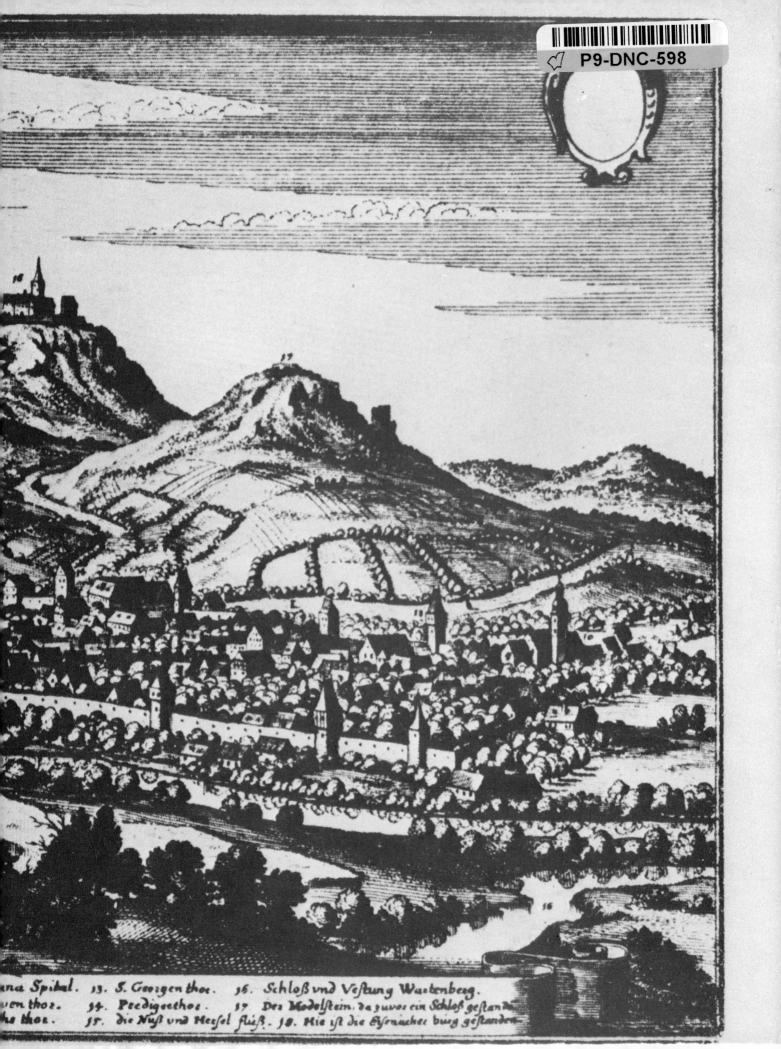

P9-DNC-598

...ana Spital. 13. S. Georgen thor. 16. Schloß vnd Vestung Wartenberg.
...ven thor. 14. Predigerthor. 17. Der Modelstein, da zuvor ein Schloß gestan..
...he thor. 15. die Nuß vnd Hessel fließ. 18. Hie ist die Ehrenacher burg gestanden.

BACH: his life and times

780.92
Bac

BACH
his life and times

Tim Dowley

Paganiniana Publications, Inc.
211 West Sylvania Avenue, Neptune City, N.J. 07753

HOWELL CARNEGIE LIBRARY
HOWELL, MICHIGAN 48843

To Mig

ISBN 0-87666-584-9

Bach: His Life and Times by Tim Dowley was originally published in 1981 by Midas Books, 12 Dene Way, Speldhurst, Tunbridge Wells, Kent TN3 0NX England. Copyright © 1981 by Dr. Tim Dowley, reprinted by permission of the publisher.

Expanded Edition of *Bach: His Life and Times* © 1981 by Paganiniana Publications, Inc. A considerable amount of new material has been added to the original text, including but not limited to illustrations and their captions. Copyright is claimed for this new material.

All rights reserved. No part of this publication may be reproduced, stored in a retrieval system, or transmitted, in any form or by any means, electronic, mechanical, photocopying, recording or otherwise without the prior permission of Midas Books and Paganiniana Publications, Inc.

Published by PAGANINIANA PUBLICATIONS, INC.
211 West Sylvania Avenue
Neptune City, New Jersey 07753

Contents

1   Beginnings: Eisenach 1685-95   7

2   A Musical Education: Ohrdruf 1695-1702   17

3   First Appointment: Arnstadt 1703-7   25

4   A Clash of Feeling: Mühlhausen 1707-8   33

5   A Court Appointment: Weimar 1708-17   41

6   Sadness and Joy: Cöthen 1717-23   53

7   The Call to Leipzig: 1723-6   67

8   Troubles in Leipzig: 1727-30   80

9   The Years of Maturity: Leipzig 1730-4   94

10 New Trials: Leipzig 1734-40   103

11 The Last Years: Leipzig 1740-50   113

    A Bach Chronology   126

    Further Reading   128

    List of Musical Works   129

    Index   143

Acknowledgements

Illustrations reproduced by kind permission of The Mansell Collection, Radio Times Hulton Picture Library and the Mary Evans Picture Library.

The author would like to acknowledge Ed Hans T David and Arthur Mendel, *The Bach Reader JM Dent*.

Former monument to Bach on the site of the Thomasschule

Johann Ambrosius Bach (1645-1695)

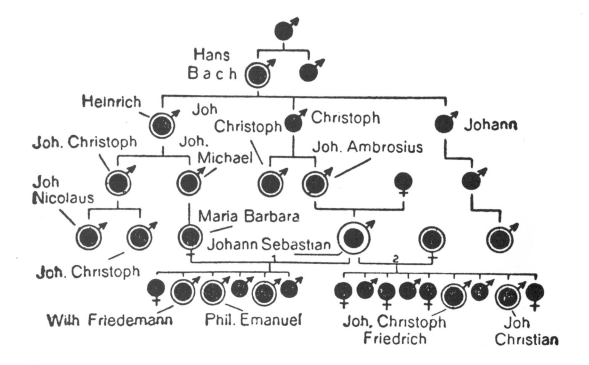

Genealogical table of the Bach family

1 Beginnings:
Eisenach 1685-95

Johann Sebastian Bach was born at Eisenach, in the region of Thuringia, 21 March 1685. By coincidence, this was little more than a month after the birth of George Frederick Handel, at Halle, about thirty miles away. Sebastian's birth is recorded in the Eisenach Church book:

March 23 1685. To Mr. Johann Ambrosius Bach, Town Musician, a son, godfathers Sebastian Nagel, Town Musician at Gotha, and Johann Georg Koch, Ducal Forester of this place. Name: Joh. Sebastian.

The Bach family had been professional musicians for several generations. In his later years, Johann Sebastian wrote proudly of

Eisenach, Thuringia

7

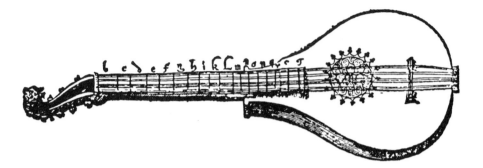

his ancestors in an account he titled the *Origin of the Bach family of Musicians.* Vitus, Sebastian's great-grandfather, had been a miller at Wechmar, near Gotha and also an accomplished zither-player. 'He found his greatest pleasure in a little zither, which he took with him even into the mill, and played while the grinding was going on.' Vitus' son, Hans, a carpet-weaver, was also an itinerant violinist. He was widely known in central Germany for his performances at wedding celebrations. Of Hans' three sons, Johannes (1604-73) was an organist and violinist, and leader of the Erfurt band; Heinrich (1615-92) was organist at Arnstadt; and Christoph (1613-61) was violinist in the Arnstadt town band. Each brother in turn produced a family of musicians; Christoph was Sebastian's grandfather. In all Sebastian numbered about forty musician-Bachs among his contemporaries; they included trumpeters, violinists, organists, choirmasters and singers.

But there was plenty to keep the professional musician busy in eighteenth-century Germany. The land was still divided up into numerous small states, dukedoms, principalities and free cities. Almost every ruler boasted his own band of court musicians; each city had its official music-makers. The court musicians would be called on to perform at ceremonial occasions, and to entertain at state functions. The municipal musicans similarly were asked to play at official functions – but were particularly needed to provide music at the town's principal church. The churches also required organists and cantors, or directors of music. All such men practised music as a craft, producing music appropriate to the occasion, with skill and practised dexterity.

Eisenach, Bach's birthplace, is famous as Luther's hide-out during his period of greatest peril, in 1531. It was here that he hid, in the hill-fortress of the Wartburg, while translating the Bible into German and writing some of his great hymns.

Sebastian's father, Johann Ambrosius, appears to have been an amiable man. Although he was not known as a composer, he was an accomplished singer, and skilled on the violin and viola. He has been described as having 'the fleshy nose and thick jaw . . . (which) seem to proclaim the stubborn tenacity of the Bach clan. His

8

Organ of the Georgenkirche in Eisenach

The Michaeliskirche in Ohrdruf

Courtyard in Bach's school in Eisenach

The Wartburg, Thuringia

shrewd eyes and dark hair complete the picture of a full-blooded, vigorous and rather earthy personality.'

Ambrosius worked as court musician for the Duke of Eisenach, playing at the castle for his patron's guests. He was also a Town Musician, and played for civic events and citizens' weddings. The people of Eisenach respected him, regarding him as a man of understanding and skill. He was married to Elizabeth, the daughter of an Erfurt councillor named Lämmerhirt; they had eight children in all. The family lived in a red-tiled two-storey house, from the top windows of which the Wartburg could be seen in the distance.

From the beginning, the young Sebastian was surrounded by music. His brothers were learning to play a variety of instruments, and the adults were constantly practising or rehearsing. He may have learned the violin from his father – and probably listened to his father's cousin, 'the profound composer' Johann Christoph, playing the organ at St George's Church.

But little is now known of Sebastian's earliest years. At the age of eight, he entered Eisenach's Latin School where two of his brothers were also pupils. He was taught Bible History, the Catechism and Latin grammar. Classes lasted from six till nine in the morning, and

9

The Bach family's home
in Eisenach

from one till three in the afternoon, with an hour extra in winter.
Sebastian did well, and evidently also had a good singing voice; he
was promoted from the choir restricted to hymn-singing to the
choir that sang motets and cantatas at St George's on Sundays.

But Sebastian's mother, Elizabeth, died on 3 May 1694, when he
was still only nine years old. Ambrosius remarried the following
January, but himself died the next month, 20 February 1695,
leaving the widow with probably five children to look after. But the
Bach family seems to have been used to supporting its members
when in such difficulties; of Ambrosius's children, Sebastian and
his brother Johann Jakob were taken into the home of their oldest
brother, Johann Christoph. This brother had been away from
Eisenach for some years, studying the organ at Erfurt with the
famous organist Johann Pachelbel. Now twenty-three, the newly-
married Johann Christoph held the post of organist at Ohrdruf,
about thirty miles from Eisenach. Just after Easter 1695, Sebastian
and Johann Jakob travelled to their new home in Ohrdruf.

Any pretence of unity within German-speaking lands had been
shattered by the turmoil of the Thirty Years' War. Petty princelings

10

and domineering dukes ruled autocratically over independent states as small as a few square miles in area. In over three hundred such states, the ruler aped the magnificence of that supreme arbitrary monarch, the Sun King, Louis XIV of France. Each strove to provide himself with a suitable palace, appropriate ceremonial and extravagant works of art – all financed largely from heavy taxation on the oppressed peasantry.

The merchants and bourgeoisie similarly puffed and preened themselves, ostentatiously seeking to project affluence and style. It was a period when commercial and dynastic prosperity was extravagantly expressed in lavish architecture, elaborate fine art, pompous powdered wigs and posturing crinolines.

Germany was riven with religious rivalries. The Catholic Church still held sway in much of southern Germany, and was rallying its strength to fight back against Protestant inroads. Over much of the remainder of Germany, Lutheranism prevailed, together with local strongholds of Reformed (or Calvinist) Protestantism. Lutheranism had petrified into a rigid dry-as-dust doctrinal system in many universities and churches, a deadness which was challenged by the

The interior of the Bachs' home, Eisenach

11

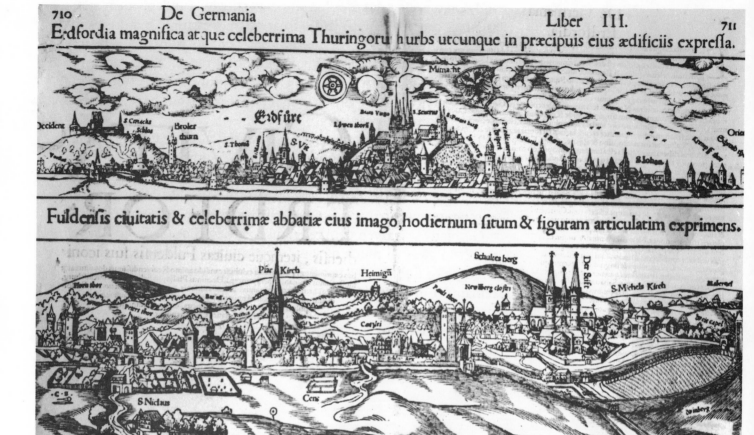

Fuldenſis ciuitatis & celeberrimæ abbatiæ eius imago, hodiernum ſitum & figuram articulatim exprimens.

Erfurt, Thuringia

warm devotion of the Pietists, who stressed the cultivation of a holy life and the imitation of Christ before all else, and gave rise to a rich vein of meditative writings.

Aware of these fissiparous tendencies, thinkers such as Leibnitz attempted to bring an intellectual unity to philosophical thought. Leibnitz's philosophical work, which posited the 'monad' as the basic constituent of all that is, gave a unifying frame to the universe.

But Germany was open to a diversity of artistic influences. Devastated by the savagery of the Thirty Years' War, there was space for cultural stimulation from abroad. Italian Baroque architecture, and the rich music of such Italian composers as Monteverdi, reached northwards to influence Catholic Austria and Bavaria. By contrast, the more sober tastes and architectural style of the prosperous Netherlanders spread south into the largely Lutheran states of northern Germany, to leave their unmistakable mark on the churches and public buildings of that area. Meanwhile, with France resurgent, the triumphant styles and forms of French architecture and painting were reflected in imitations and influences throughout Germany.

Germany stood at the crossroads of musical influences too. She had her own tradition of polyphonic singing, the heritage of the

Louis XIV, *Le Roi Soleil*

12

14

Middle Ages and of the Lutheran Reformation. From Italy in music, as in art and architecture, there travelled a distinctive set of styles: melodies of sensual charm and dramatic strength; the unique tradition of *bel canto* singing. From Italy, too, came the musical forms of the concerto, featuring one or more solo instrument, and the trio sonata, in which two instruments played melodically, while the third provided a bass, and a keyboard instrument filled in the harmonies.

The French contribution in music was equally clear; in France there first appeared the overture, with its order of slow introduction, quick fugue and emphatic coda, as well as the dance suite, made up of a series of different dance-types, and programme music, with its attempts to describe musically natural phenomena or events. The French also led the rest of Europe in techniques of orchestral organisation and performance.

While some German musicians preferred one style to another, gradually the various influences were combined and assimilated to produce the rich musical style characteristic of late Baroque, in the first part of the eighteenth century.

A concert for aristocrats in
eighteenth-century France

2 A Musical Education: Ohrdruf, 1695-1702

Life was not easy at Ohrdruf. Johann Christian soon had a child of of his own to support, as well as his two younger brothers, all on the slim stipend received from the City Council for his duties as organist. Johann Jakob left Ohrdruf only a year later, to become apprentice to the new town musician back in Eisenach.

Sebastian was able to help support his brother's family. He had a fine, penetrating voice of good range and was able to earn good fees for performing. But he also continued his studies at Ohrdruf, attending the well-known Latin school, and achieving precocious results. Not only was he instructed in Latin, as the school's title would suggest, but also in orthodox Lutheran beliefs, which offered him another area to exercise his intellectual virtuosity. He later built up a sizeable collection of theological works to be read at his leisure.

But Sebastian was by no means deprived of musical stimulus. His brother, Johann Christoph, an artist of the first rank, continued the work begun at Eisenach. He was responsible for instructing Sebastian in playing the clavier, and allowed his younger brother to watch carefully as a new organ was constructed and installed at the town's church. He almost certainly assisted further Sebastian's efforts at composition, and helped him master other musical instruments.

A famous, but possibly apocryphal, story dates from this period. If true, it illustrates the youthful musicians's thirst for knowledge. Apparently Sebastian was denied access by his brother to a manuscript he possessed of clavier compositions by such accomplished composers as Böhm, Buxtehude, Pachelbel and Fosberger. Sebastian is supposed to have surreptitiously removed it from a forbidden bookcase, copied it out by moonlight, to avoid detection, and stealthily replaced the original. To Sebastian's chagrin, when Johann Christoph discovered the painstaking copy, he confiscated it. Such a story seems to run counter to what we

Johann Christoph Bach
(1732-95)

17

18

know of the relationship between the musical brothers; Sebastian in due course dedicated a clavier piece to Johann Christoph, and later took two of his sons into his own home to give them a musical education.

Whatever the truth of the story, the Ohrdruf household was soon unable to contain Sebastian any longer. Johann Christoph now had two children of his own, and at the age of fifteen Sebastian left Ohrdruf school, for lack of funds. None of the other Bachs was in a position to be able to offer him a musical apprenticeship.

But a new opportunity opened up in Lüneberg, two hundred miles to the north. Sebastian only heard about it because a new music teacher at Ohrdruf, Elias Herda, had studied at Lüneberg, and described the exceptional little group of singers which made up the boy's choir (*Mettenchor*) at St Michael's Church there. The great attraction for Sebastian was that choir members, who earned a small stipend together with free board and instruction, had to be the offspring of poor people, with nothing to live on, but possessing good voices. Normally the choir was looking for younger boys, or for those whose voices had already broken. But evidently Herda provided such a glowing account of Sebastian's ability that he was granted a scholarship.

Lüneberg

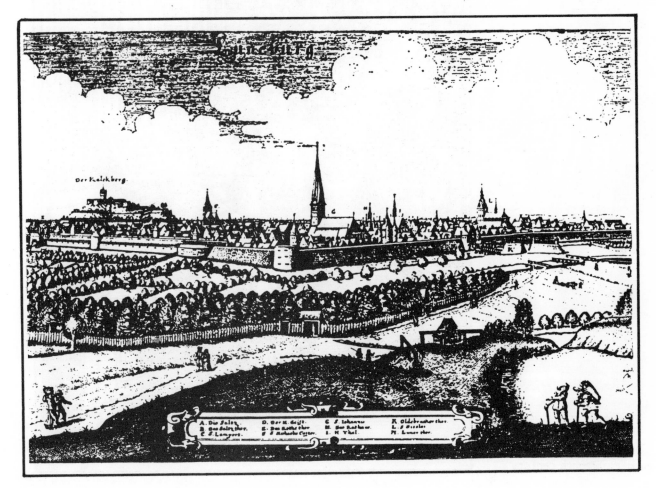

So it was that in March 1700 Sebastian set out on the 200-mile trek to Lüneberg, accompanied by an older schoolfriend, Georg Erdmann, whose voice had already broken. When he arrived,

Church musicians in the early eighteenth century

20

Sebastian was able to continue his academic studies as a pupil of St Michael's Latin school, as well as taking a full part in the musical life of the church. Again the curriculum included Latin and Greek, logic, rhetoric and religion. Although his monthly allowance as a member of the *Mettenchor* was a mere twelve groschen, he was able to supplement this with his earnings as a singer at weddings and funerals, and as a street performer.

The musical and artistic traditions of St Michael's were most impressive. The church itself was awe-inspiring, with its towering nave and vaulting. Its high altar was widely known for its rich gold centre and its enamel decoration; and the music was equally lavish. Since the mid-sixteenth century, when the first Protestant Cantor had been established, a music library had been built up at St Michael's. The great Cantor Friedrich Emanuel Praetorius (1623-95) had added many important musical manuscripts and printed editions, and at his death the catalogue included 1102 titles, representing the work of some 175 composers.

With such riches of repertoire to draw upon, and with such a good choir, St Michael's developed a fine musical tradition. Sebastian became acquainted with a vast amount of church music, both through his listening and his singing. Although his voice broke soon after arriving at Lüneberg, he was retained as a scholarship boy and was probably also called on to assist the three instrumentalists at the church on his violin – or even at the organ.

Hamburg in the late eighteenth century

As at Ohrdruf, Sebastian had the opportunity to investigate the mechanical functioning of the organ, when the St Michael's instrument underwent restoration. The work was expertly done in 1701 by the organ-builder Johann Balthasar Herd, who had been responsible for similar work on the renowned organs at Lübeck and Hamburg.

Louis XIV dressed as 'Sun King' for a masque

But possibly the most important encounter Sebastian had at Lüneberg was with Georg Böhm, organist at St John's Church. Böhm, who was also a considerable composer, would have known the Bach family from his own youth in Thuringia. Bach certainly listened to Böhm performing – and it seems difficult to believe that he did not take the opportunity to make his closer acquaintance. Böhm's influence is clear in some of Sebastian's early organ music.

The network of influences continues. Böhm, in turn, owed much to his teacher, the accomplished organist J. A. Reinken, who still played at St Catherine's, Hamburg, although in his seventy-eighth year. Sebastian must have been greatly impressed by Böhm's reports, since he took the opportunity of the summer holiday of

Francois Couperin (1668-1733) the French composer

1701 to walk the thirty miles to Hamburg. Not only did he listen to Reinken at his organ, but he also took this opportunity to listen to another renowned North German organist, Vincenz Lübeck, and possibly also to visit the Hamburg Opera House. So impressed was the young musician that he repeated this trip on several occasions.

Back in Lüneberg, Bach was also coming up against French cultural influences. The *Ritterakademie,* the school for young aristocrats attached to St Michael's, was taking up fashionable French ideas; the students conversed in French, put on French drama, and even had a one-time pupil of Lully, Thomas de la Salle, as dance instructor, to the accompaniment of French music.

Sebastian familiarised himself with the French language, with French plays – and most importantly with French music. De la Salle was impressed enough with Bach to take him with him to the city of Celle, where he also worked as Court Musician to the Duke of Brunswick-Lüneberg, Georg Wilhelm. With a permanent orchestra of sixteen musicians, de la Salle was attempting to bring to the court the fashionable French style; refugee Huguenots and other French musicians provided a high standard of performance, and were amply rewarded for their labours by the artistic Duke.

On his visits to Celle, the young Bach would have listened to French organ music performed on the little organ in the castle chapel, and heard keyboard and orchestral works by such great French composers as Couperin. His copies of suites by composers including Nicolas de Grigny and Charles Dieupart betray his early delight in French keyboard music.

Sebastian seems to have taken every opportunity to extend his musical experience during his time in Lüneberg. His precocity is perhaps illustrated by his determination to explore a variety of different avenues – rather than narrowly restrict himself to a single enthusiasm. But by Easter 1702 he had completed his academic studies at St Michael's. The next step would have been university; but without the necessary funds, university was never a real option for him. In any event, at the age of seventeen, Sebastian was anxious to pursue his musical career.

Jan Adams Reinken (1623-1722)

Jan Adams Reinken,
famous organist of the
Katherinenkirche in Hamburg

The palace at Celle

Bach as a young man

Neue Kirche, Arnstadt

3 First Appointment:
Arnstadt 1703-7

Sebastian decided to return to home territory for his first musical post. He travelled back to Thuringia, only to find organists' posts vacant at Sangerhausen, at Arnstadt and at Eisenach. As well as the solace of being near to his roots, he could probably rely on the family name, and possibly influence, to help him find a position in Thuringia.

The Sangerhausen Council voted unanimously for the young Bach to be invited to be organist at St James' Church; but the local ruler, the Duke of Sachsen-Weissenfels, objected to the appointment of such an inexperienced youth, and had his own candidate, Johann Augustin Kobelius, appointed instead. The Eisenach opening also went to another – a more renowned Bach, Johann Bernhard.

The situation at Arnstadt was a little complicated. A new church of St Boniface had been built some twenty years earlier to replace a previous building destroyed by fire, and the new single-manual organ was still not ready for use. In the meantime, Sebastian found employment as 'lackey and violinist' in the little orchestra of Johann Ernst, the artistic younger brother of the Duke of Weimar, and also acted as assistant to the elderly court organist, Johann

Arnstadt

Effler. While employed by Ernst, Sebastian probably performed some of the Italian music then coming into vogue.

Sebastian's chance finally came when the Mayor of Arnstadt, a distant relative, persuaded the City Council to invite him to test their newly-completed church organ:

Upon the command of the Consistory of the Council, Mr Johann Sebastian Bach . . . was summoned here to inspect the new organ in the New Church.
Arnstadt July 13 1703.

As he had hoped, this opened up the way for Sebastian's appointment as organist at Arnstadt. His performance at the organ tests must have been extraordinarily impressive. Normally several candidates were put through their paces before the victor was chosen; in this case Sebastian was the only organist considered, and a month later he took up his duties. His contract stipulated he should:

appear promptly on Sundays, feast days, and other days of divine service in the New Church at the organ entrusted to you; to play it suitably; to keep a watchful eye over it and take good care of it; to report in good time if part of it becomes weak, and give warning to get the necessary repairs done; not to allow access to it to anyone without the knowledge of the Superintendent; generally to ensure that damage is avoided and everything kept in good order. Also, in your daily life cultivate the fear of God, sobriety and love of peace; completely avoid bad company and anything which distracts you from your calling, generally conducting yourself as towards God in all respects . . .

For all this solemn warning, the duties were not onerous. Sebastian was only required to play three days a week; on Sundays from eight till ten in the morning; on Mondays at the service of intercession; and on Thursday mornings. Apart from this, he was expected to organise a small choir from boys at the Latin school, although this was not spelt out in his contract. Arnstadt had no Cantor, and the duties he would have exercised devolved upon Sebastian.

Arnstadt, with its population of 3,800, was a pleasant city, with an abundance of lime trees, richly-flowered gardens landscaping the castle surrounds, a Renaissance Town Hall and the Romanesque Church of Our Lady. The ruler, Anton Günther II, had a sparkling court, with a Paul Gleitsmann to direct his orchestra, to which, doubtless, Sebastian contributed his services.

Sebastian also took the opportunity to renew friendship with some of his own family living nearby. He was particularly attracted to Maria Barbara, the youngest daughter of Johann Michael Bach, the late organist at Gehten. The two orphans both lived for a time with their mutual relative, Martin Feldhaus, the Mayor of Arnstadt, at the House of the Golden Crown. They were sufficiently distant relatives for this to provide no obstacle to the plans they began to formulate for marriage.

But Sebastian's time at Arnstadt was not all love idylls. A young man, he experienced discipline problems in his role as choirmaster, and in turn had insufficient maturity to deal with the rebukes he attracted for his own misbehaviour.

The choir proved to be more than he had the experience or patience to cope with. They were poor singers – the other two city

A bassoon player

Market place and St Mary's Church, Lübeck

churches had cornered the more accomplished musicians – and the choristers were liable to behave in 'a scandalous manner'. Sebastian's temper got the better of him more than once, notably in his dealings with a bassoonist named Gegenbach. Eventually the mutual animosity grew to such an extent that the two fell into a street brawl in the course of which Sebastian drew his sword, tearing to tatters his enemy's clothes. Bach went to the church authorities to complain about the student's behaviour – but was not heard entirely sympathetically, since his bad relations with the choir were already common currency in the city. They recognised that the material he had to deal with was far from ideal, but urged him to persevere. Sebastian was recalcitrant, and began to neglect his non-contractual responsibilities for the choir.

Not long after matters had erupted over Gegenbach, Sebastian requested four weeks' leave of absence from Arnstadt to visit Lübeck, to hear the celebrated organist at St Mary's, Dietrich Buxtehude. The Arnstadt authorities released him, accepting as a locum his cousin, Johann Ernst. The particular ambition Sebastian wanted to fulfil was to hear the five Sunday evening programmes of music which Buxtehude planned for the season of Advent.

29

In addition to the regular church choir of St Mary's, forces of forty instrumentalists, arranged on four platforms, contributed to the impressive occasion. Sebastian was captivated; he was even able to attend a special performance occasioned by the death of the Emperor Leopold I, and by the accession of the new Emperor.

So excited was the young man that he failed to return home after his permitted four weeks – or even to write to ask for an extension of leave. The weeks stretched on; but he was taken up with Buxtehude's art. Four weeks became four months. Even now Bach was reluctant to return to Arnstadt; he called on Reichlin in Hamburg and Böhm at Lüneberg before arriving back in Arnstadt in January 1706. Nor did he apologise.

The congregation at Arnstadt now received further shocks. The young organist brought back with him new ideas. His hymn accompaniments were unrecognisable to their conservative ears; he added new-fangled ornamentation, counter-melody, extraordinary harmonies and strange passages between verses.

Bach's behaviour could only lead to formal complaints; he was called before the church authorities in February 1706:

Complaints have been made to the Consistory that you now accompany the hymns with surprising variations and irrelevant ornaments, which obliterate the melody and confuse the congregation. . . . We are surprised that you have given up performing music for voices and instruments, and assume that this is due to your bad relations with the pupils at the Latin school. We must therefore ask you to tell us explicitly that you are ready to rehearse them in music for voices and instruments as well as in the hymns. We cannot provide a Cantor, and you must tell us clearly, yes or no, whether you will do as we ask. If you will not, we must find an organist who will.

Bach faced an ultimatum: he must mend his ways or look for another position. But in fact he made no great rush to decide what to do. The authorities were in effect restricting his more adventurous playing in favour of safe conservatism; he was told, for instance, not to confuse the congregation by straying rapidly from one strange key into another. But he could now do no right; whereas previously he had been criticised for his overlong and overly complex preludes, now they were declared too short. In November 1706, Sebastian received another severe reprimand:

The organist Bach . . . must declare whether or not he is willing to make music with the scholars as already instructed; if he considers it no disgrace to be linked with the church and receive a salary, he must not be ashamed to make music with the students assigned, until directed otherwise.

Clearly dismissal would follow unless Sebastian improved his

The Bach organ in the
Church of St Boniface,
Arnstadt

record. But the criticism became even more personal. A young
woman had been heard singing to Sebastian's accompaniment in
the organ gallery. Tongues soon gossipped, and this 'scandal' was
reported to the church authorities. Sebastian was again asked to
explain his behaviour. It is possible that the woman in question was
his cousin, Maria Barbara, who seems to have provided him with
the warm understanding he needed in this period of stress.

But matters were not all so painful. Sebastian was evidently busy

31

composing during these years. When his brother Johann Jakob took up a military career, entering the service of King Charles XII of Sweden as an oboist in his army, Sebastian wrote a light-hearted *Capriccio on the departure of his beloved brother*, in which he painted musically friends dissuading his brother from leaving, the 'various calamities which might overtake him in foreign lands' and even the postilion horn.

But clearly Sebastian's days at Arnstadt were numbered. He could not restrain his musical ambition indefinitely at the orders of conservative town officers – nor endure the purgatory of training a choir of rebel spirits.

King Charles XII of Sweden

4 A Clash of Feeling:
Mühlhausen 1707-8

With things so difficult at Arnstadt, Sebastian began to investigate alternative openings. Once again the way seemed favourable. In December 1706 the famous composer and organist at St Blaise's Church, in the Free Imperial City of Mühlhausen, Johann Georg Ahle, died. Sebastian's skills were becoming more widely known; he was invited to visit Mühlhausen for a trial performance on the organ on Easter Day 1707. One of the councillors at Mühlhausen, Johann Bellstedt, was related to Maria Barbara, and liaised with Sebastian on arrangements.

So impressed with his virtuosity were the authorities at Mühlhausen, that Sebastian was summoned to discuss terms. He was able to extract a salary greater than that of his predecessor, by demanding parity with his stipend at Arnstadt. In addition, he was to receive fifty-four bushels of grain, two cords of wood, and a large quantity of faggots. In due course the Burgomaster of Mühlhausen sent him a formal contract, which was ratified by Sebastian's handshake on 15 June 1707.

Sebastian now moved quickly. Without further rancour, he informed the Arnstadt church of his call, requested his dismissal, and was granted permission to hand back the organ keys. (This was

Mühlhausen

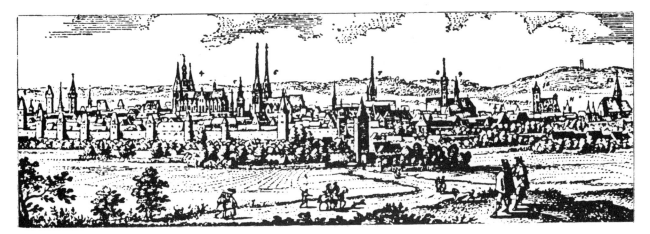

33

not always a mere formality; many an organist's career had been blocked by his employer's refusal to accept his resignation.) He was replaced at Arnstadt by a relative, his cousin Johann Ernst Bach – but on only half Sebastian's salary. Sebastian himself was now free to commence duties at Mühlhausen.

But he returned once again to Arnstadt – this time for a pleasurable occasion. Financially he was now in a position to be able to marry Maria Barbara. In August 1707 Sebastian's uncle, Tobias Lämmerhirt, died, leaving him a small legacy of fifty gulders. The marriage of Sebastian and Maria Barbara took place on 17 October 1707, at the village church of Dornheim, conducted by the pastor Johann Lorenz Stauber, a friend of the family. Still only twenty-three, Sebastian's early marriage was entirely in keeping with family custom. Certainly it seems to have provided the security and company – and probably musical interest – which he needed to encourage him in his efforts.

After a few days spent with relatives in Erfurt, the newly-weds proceeded to Mühlhausen to set up home and build their new life. The position Sebastian held at St Blaise's was considerably more prestigious than that at the third church at Arnstadt. The beautiful building, with its dignified twin spires, was an admirable setting for his music-making, and he followed several illustrious organists at the church. At last he had the freedom and opportunity to display the latent enthusiasms and ambitions built up in Arnstadt and previously.

Although his formal contract only required Sebastian to play at the services, he took on much wider responsibilities, trying to bring new life to the musical diet of the city. At St Blaise's he felt the type of music which Ahle had performed was rather restricting: mainly fairly straightforward chorale-type arias, with instrumental refrains (or ritornellos). Bach was keen to introduce cantatas like those by Buxtehude and the musicians of North Germany.

To enable him to introduce this new repertoire, Sebastian and his pupil Johann Martin Schubart busied themselves copying works for the church music-library. He was also active musically in the surrounding village churches; he was even incautious enough to tell the Mühlhausen authorities that he sometimes preferred the village musicians.

Sebastian was called on to provide music for the annual inauguration of the City Council, which occurred at the magnificent St Mary's Church. For this occasion he composed a cantata in the style of Buxtehude, dividing his orchestra into four sections. The large-scale work, entitled 'God is our King', impressed his patrons sufficiently for it to be published following its first performance in February 1708.

Bach now came into his own as an experienced organist; he was

Details of the way an eighteenth-century organ was constructed

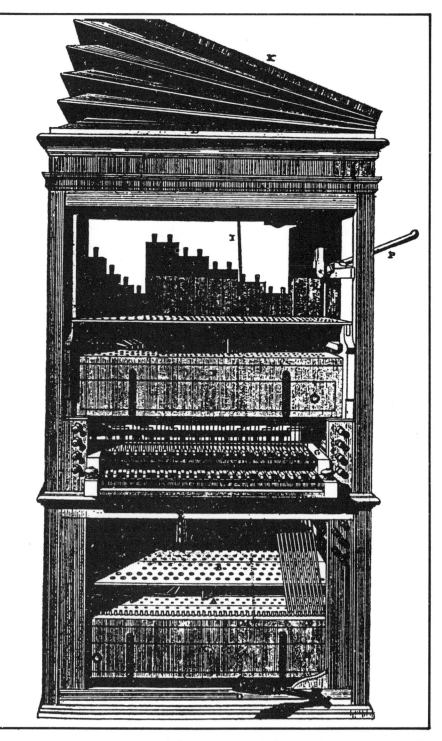

able to oversee the repair of the rather defective instrument at St Blaise's. He first made a careful inspection of the organ, noting meticulously the defects and faults in its various components:

The lack of wind must be compensated by adding three good new bellows . . . The trombone bass must be supplied with new larger pipes, and the mouthpieces quite differently arranged to give this stop a more solid tone . . .

The trumpet will be taken out and a fagotto . . . installed, useful for all sorts of new ideas, and which sounds fine in music for voices and instruments.

Sebastian went into technical detail on how to go about making the necessary repairs, and how to modify the organ. He evidently based much of his instructions on the organ at St George's, Eisenach, which had been restored under the supervision of Johann

Paul Gerhardt (1605-75), Pietist hymn writer and theologian

Christoph Bach. Sebastian's specifications meant that the organ would acquire a third manual, and more bellows, giving the potential for greater contrast in volume and in tone colouring. As a novelty, he also stipulated the construction of a set of chimes operated by the pedal; these were evidently included on the special request of the parishioners, and at their expense.

The parish authorities at Mühlhausen had great confidence in their young organist's technical ability; they accepted his report, and asked him to have the work put in hand. The organ-builder employed was to be offered a small organ in the choir loft if the 200-thaler payment was insufficient to cover his fee.

Despite his musical achievements, Bach encountered controversy again at Mühlhausen. On this occasion the problem was theological; the pastor at St Blaise's, J. A. Frohne, was a Pietist, stressing the devotional, subjective aspects of the Christian life, in reaction to the sometimes extreme intellectualism and dryness of some orthodox Lutheran theologians. The Pietists thirsted for spirituality, for holiness, for revival; they feared the excessive use of music and art in worship, with its temptations to worldliness. Some Pietists wanted a complete ban on instrumental music; 'sirensongs disturbing meditation, mixing the world's vanity with the sacred, and corrupting the gold of divine truth'.

In such a climate, Sebastian's musical innovations, which had already shocked the pious at Arnstadt as florid and confusing, were decidedly unwelcome. His predecessor, Ahle, had laboured conservatively for thirty-three years; Sebastian's reforms were attacked as worldly and carnal. Inevitably the young musician found such criticisms hard to take

But he became involved theologically too. Sebastian's own education was staunchly orthodox, and he sympathised with the orthodox pastor of St Mary's Church, G. C. Eilmar, who was in fierce doctrinal conflict with Frohne. Bach certainly took no part in this conflict, but his loyalties were probably torn between Eilmar and the personal expression of devotion favoured by the Pietists. What he could never tolerate was their outlawing of complex, profound musical performance.

Although Sebastian continued to display an interest in orthodox theology, adding regularly to his library of doctrinal works, his choice of texts for many of his cantatas displays an equal enthusiasm for the sentiments of Pietism, with its stress on the sufferings of Christ, and the yearning for heaven. Although Eilmar was a dogged opponent of the pastor of St Blaise's, he encouraged the organist at his rival's church, writing libretti for his cantatas, and commissioning new works. Sebastian was impressed with Eilmar's support, and later invited the pastor to act as godfather to his first child, born in December 1708, at Weimar.

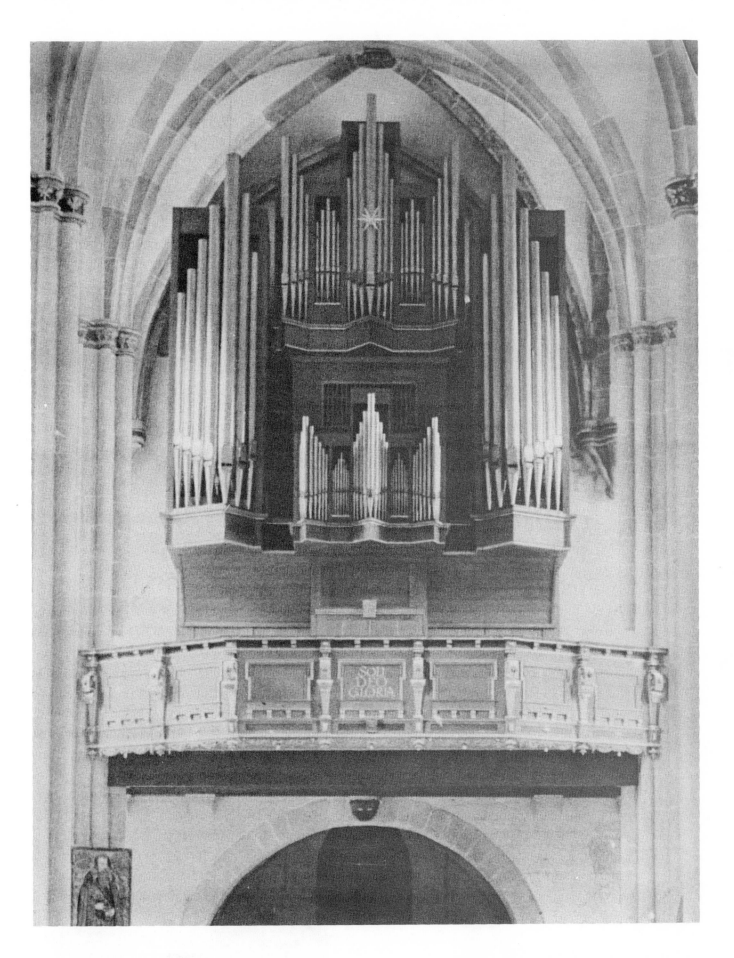

Organ of the Blasiuskirche, Mulhausen

Johann Adolf Frohne

Georg Christian Eilmar

But Sebastian was sufficiently unsettled to look for another move. There was not room for his talents in the church of a Pietist pastor such as Frohne. Once again the way ahead became clear: Bach received an invitation from Wilhelm Ernst, Duke of Saxe-Weimar, to join his court as a chamber musician and organist. He would replace the aged and infirm Johann Effler, providing largely liturgical music for his patron. Sebastian travelled to Weimar to give a trial performance in June 1708, and, when accepted, wrote a polite letter resigning his post at St Blaise's:

I have not been allowed to do my work without opposition, and at present there is not the least appearance that things will improve . . . Moreover, if I may say so respectfully, modest as is my way of life, I have not enough to live on, with the payment of rent, and the purchase of essential goods.

In spite of these carping notes, Sebastian evidently maintained overall good relations with Mühlhausen; he continued to supervise the organ repairs even after taking up his new duties at Weimar.

It will be useful to take a moment to discuss why Bach's music sounded unacceptable to the Mühlhausen congregation – and why for us it contrasts equally with his great successors such as Mozart and Beethoven and the nineteenth-century romantic composers. A major distinction lies in the style of writing.

Bach was composing in the Baroque style. He was concerned to sustain simultaneous melodic lines in various parts, in the form known as counterpoint. This contrasted with the basically harmonic style which appeared later in the eighteenth century.

Since there was an emphasis on maintaining the same lines of counterpoint throughout a particular piece of music, there was no attempt to vary the mood or emotional pitch during its course. The Baroque style was governed by the contemporary 'Doctrine of the Affections', which included emotions, such as joy, anger and grief,

An eighteenth-century
musical instrument maker

but also states of mind. In the late Baroque period, each affection would be expressed by a particular rhythm, melody or harmonic pattern – or all three. In addition, instruments too came to be linked to particular 'affections': oboes and flutes to the pastoral; trumpets and timpani to the royal, horns to the pompous, and so forth. This approach was certainly never a mere mechanical system in the hands of so imaginative a composer as Bach, as any serious listener will know.

In these early years, Sebastian's own compositions were strongly influenced by his contemporaries and predecessors. Often he would copy out in entirety works which he particularly admired, and these included music by other members of the Bach family, as well as those by French, Italian and other German composers. His compositions are often experimental – he was trying to work out new ideas, and new approaches and emotional feelings – but often the music becomes lengthy and unstructured.

During his time at Arnstadt and Mühlhausen, the young Sebastian was already composing in a variety of musical forms: the sonata, toccata, capriccio, prelude and fugue, chorale prelude and cantata. The early cantatas are closely modelled on those of such composers as Pachelbel, Böhm and Buxtehude of the North German tradition. They are simply constructed, with musical settings of Bible texts or hymns, with short sections in various tempos, and for various voices.

Bach's first cantata was written while he was still only nineteen: *Denn du wirst meine Seele* ('Suffer not Thou my soul . . .'). Of the unknown number of cantatas which he wrote at Mühlhausen, we have already mentioned that composed for the new City Council, *Gott ist mein König* ('God is my King') with its orchestration for brass ensemble, two woodwind ensembles, and a string section, as well as two separate choirs.

Among the finest of Sebastian's early works was his cantata *Gottes Zeit* ('God's own Time'), with its theme of the transformation of man's hope through the coming of Christ and his new era. The text was probably put together by Sebastian himself from hymns and the Bible; he used inspired instrumental writing and dramatic vocal composition to create a work of great emotional intensity.

With organ music, too, his early works are those of an apprentice, exploring all the potentialities of his chosen craft, displaying heightened emotions and great vigour. He wrote many free-running preludes and toccatas, often deriving their brilliant style from his admired masters, Buxtehude and Böhm. Similarly, his clavier works of these years were influenced by contemporaries, in this case largely by composers of southern and central Germany. We have already noticed his playful Capriccio, written to mark Johann Christoph's departure to join the Swedish army.

Manuscript page from the cantata "Gott ist mein Konig"

Wilhelm Ernst, Duke of Saxe-Weimar

5 A Court Appointment: Weimar 1708-17

By moving forty miles to Weimar, Sebastian moved into a completely different social world. His salary was immediately almost doubled, and his religious problems at Mühlhausen were left far behind. A fervent Lutheran, Duke Wilhelm Ernst was also an enthusiastic musical patron.

Bach's position was one of considerable prestige. As organist and chamber musician, Sebastian was expected to dress himself in

Weimar

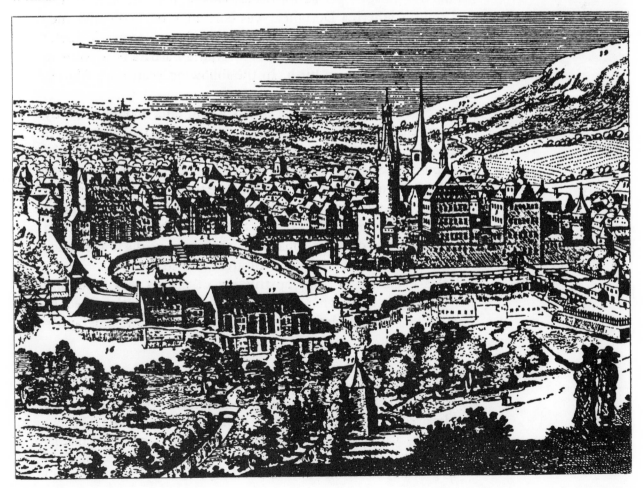

Hungarian Haiduk uniform when he played his violin. But he also found this an atmosphere conducive to composing. The Duke would allow none of the religious rancour that marked Sebastian's time at Mühlhausen; the organist was free to develop his ideas on 'well-regulated church music', and during his nine years in Weimar composed most of his best works for the organ.

Duke Wilhelm Ernst's religious enthusiasm was not merely formal; he personally supervised daily devotions at court, when his servants were required in turn to read from the Bible. He would catechise his staff on the subject-matter of the sermon, and encouraged a sober, restrained pattern of life. While economising on such suspect entertainments as theatre and dancing, the Duke arranged for daily cut-flowers to be available, and put money aside for charitable purposes. His frugal, simple tastes contrasted with the extravagant pomp of many of his contemporaries.

Despite these puritanical leanings, the Duke was despotic in his exercise of authority. He brooked no questioning of his will, and it was fortunate for Sebastian that the Duke did not enforce his will musically. Though the Duke no longer allowed opera at court, he whole-heartedly encouraged concerts in the Baroque chapel.

This was a happy period for Sebastian's family. Maria Barbara's first child, Catherina Dorothea, was born in 1708, soon after they arrived in Weimar. Then, two years later, came Wilhelm Friedemann, born 22 November 1710. Maria Barbara bore twins in 1713, but both died on birth. In the following year, on 8 March, Carl Philipp Emanuel was born.

The organ in the court chapel was small, and, though recently reconstructed, Sebastian persuaded the Duke to modify it yet further. He got his patron to have it fitted with a set of chimes like those put in at St Blaise's, and then managed to have the instrument completely reconstructed again. This time the work was undertaken by Heinrich Trebs, an organ-builder in whom Sebastian had great faith. In 1711 he provided Trebs with a Testimonial, declaring him 'a reasonable and conscientious man, for he gave us the lowest price and then did the work agreed with great industry'.

Bach's expertise on the construction of organs was becoming increasingly well-known and used. He was frequently asked to examine or test deficient or repaired instruments. One biographer records:

He was severe, but always fair, in his trials of organs. As he was perfectly acquainted with the construction of the instrument, he could not be in any way deceived. The first thing he did in trying out an organ was to pull out all the stops and play with the full organ. He used to say in jest that he must know whether the instrument had good lungs. After the examination . . . he generally entertained himself and those present by showing his skill

Prince Ernst August of Saxe-Weimar

Das Fürstliche Sächsische Palatium und Residentz zu Weimar wie solches von Ihre Fürstlichen Gnaden, Herzog Wilhelmen zu Sachsen Anno 1650. bis 1654. erbauet worden.

The Wilhelmsburg Palace in Weimar

The Schlosskirche, Weimar

as a performer . . . He would choose some theme and execute it in all the
various forms of organ composition, never changing his theme, even
though he might play, without intermission, for two hours or more. First
he used it for a prelude and a fugue, with the full organ. Then he showed
his facility at using the stops for a trio, a quartet, and so on. Afterwards
there followed a chorale, the melody of which was playfully surrounded in
the most diversified manner . . .

On the strength of his reputation, Sebastian was often invited to
perform on the organ in neighbouring cities. A notable instance was
on the impressive organ at the Church of Our Lady at Halle. He
was intrigued with the 65-stop organ installed there, when visiting
Halle, and responded to an invitation by the pastor to perform the
customary test-piece. For this occasion, not only did Sebastian
make the requisite performance, but also wrote a special cantata,
probably *Ich hatte viel Bekümmerhis* ('I had much distress'), later
performed at Weimar. The libretto was almost certainly provided
by Salomo Franck, Court Librarian to Duke Wilhelm Ernst.

43

Halle, Saxony

Sebastian was tempted to move once again when the organist's post at Halle fell vacant. The 'Council of Eight' at the Halle church were immediately attracted by the idea, and drew up a lengthy offer for the position. They laid down a whole host of questions, conditions and requirements; but it was finally the low salary which apparently proved the biggest stumbling block for Sebastian. It was less than he was receiving at Weimar – where his salary had improved considerably during his years there. While Sebastian lingered over his decision, the Duke raised his salary again, clinching his organist's resolve to stay at Weimar. This annoyed the electors of Halle; they accused Sebastian of negotiating with them merely to coerce his employer into raising his salary. The Duke now raised his organist to the position of Choirmaster (1714) 'for which he is obliged to perform new works monthly'.

At the same time, Sebastian wrote to the Church Board at Halle, rejecting strongly any idea that he had acted in an underhand fashion: 'I do not have to journey to Halle in order to have my salary increased'. Fortunately his arguments – or time – healed this breach. When the Halle organ was finally completed in 1716, Sebastian was invited, along with the organists Christian Friedrich Rolle and Johann Kuhnau, to test it. He jumped at the opportunity, and carried out the work conscientiously.

The report on the organ of the Church of Our Lady covered every aspect:

Johann Sebastian Bach

We found the bellows-chamber big enough for the bellows, and well-protected against adverse weather conditions; but we also noted that since

44

45

the window faces west, the bellows are exposed to excessive sun; a curtain or some other protection from the sun will be necessary when the organ is not in use . . . With the wind-chests we found no visible defects, and they stood up to the test of having the keys of the manual and pedal keyboards pressed down at the same time without our discovering any leaks except a little in the middle manual; this is caused by the upper boards being screwed too loosely, and can easily be remedied.

They even referred to the outer appearance of the organ:

The pipes forming the organ's facade ought to shine brightly; presumably the best of the good tin was used for them. The fact that they do not shine is not the fault of the builder, but is caused by soot falling on them

The organ examiners were entertained royally by the Church Board. On the dedication of the new organ at Halle, Sunday 3 May 1716, a banquet of impressive proportions was served, with the following menu:

Boeuf à la mode
Pike with anchovy butter sauce
Smoked ham
Peas, potatoes, spinach and chicory
Roast mutton.
Warm asparagus salad
Boiled pumpkin
Lettuce
Roast Veal
Fritters
Radishes
Candied lemon peel
Preserved cherries
Fresh butter

Sebastian's musical activities at Weimar broadened considerably with his promotion to the new post of Choirmaster. While the old bandmaster's son, Johann Wilhelm Drese, provided what secular music was required at court, Sebastian guaranteed to supply a new cantata every month. It was for such reasons that this period was Sebastian's most fertile for organ composition. He seems to have simultaneously reached a peak of virtuosity as both a performer and as a composer for the 'king of instruments'.

His skills were rapidly becoming legendary. We have a contemporary description of a recital Sebastian gave at Cassel for the Crown Prince:

His feet flew over the pedal-board as if winged, and powerful notes roared like thunder through the church. Frederick, the Crown Prince, was filled with such amazement and admiration that he took a ring set with precious

EFFIGIES ANTONII VIVALDI

Antonio Vivaldi (1675? – 1741), the Italian composer

stones from his finger and gave it to Bach immediately the music died away.

As Choirmaster at Weimar, Sebastian had a trained group of singers and instrumentalists at his disposal, and was able to build up experience as conductor as well as composer. The musical forces at his disposal included a bassoon, six trumpets, kettledrums, two tenors, two basses, two sopranos, three violins and six boy choristers. Sebastian, as conductor, would lead the other musicians with his own violin, both rehearsals and performances taking place in the court chapel.

In his years at Weimar, Bach was still interesting himself widely in what other composers had done. He particularly studied the Italians, often adapting their string concertos as solos for harpsichord or organ. He arranged at least six Vivaldi violin concertos for harpsichord, and three for the organ. From the southern composers, Sebastian developed a proficiency for sensitive melody, and found a great warmth and intensity.

Bach wrote a large number of cantatas at Weimar to fulfil his contractual obligations as Choirmaster. Some of the Weimar cantatas reveal a great sympathy for to the mystical, almost Pietist, texts which he often chose to set. The mystery of death and the hope of resurrection drew from him a subjective and expressive strain of great beauty; the title of Cantata 161, *Komm du süsse Todesstunde* ('Come sweet death, thou blessed healer') reveals this mystical note. What is probably the final cantata composed at Weimar, *Christ lag in Todesbanden* ('Christ lay by death unshrouded') was simply a setting of a rugged sixteenth-century hymn by the great reformer himself, Martin Luther.

But Bach's cantatas were not solely written for church use. He wrote a number for various secular occasions, such as birthdays, weddings, and, later, for special events at the University of Leipzig. These often more relaxed pieces gave Sebastian the opportunity to display his love of nature and his fairly basic sense of humour.

It is difficult to quantify the total of such pieces, since Sebastian tended to re-use material which he felt was particularly successful. Often ideas first worked out for his secular cantatas in due course re-appeared in sacred works; for Bach there was nothing improper in such a careful stewardship of materials, or in the use of secular material for Christian occasions.

It was during this time at Weimar that Sebastian wrote the beautiful and familiar aria 'Sheep may safely graze' as the pastorale for his secular cantata *Was mir behagt ist nur die muntre Jagd* ('The merry chase, the hunt, is my delight').

As already noted, it is in his organ works that he first reached maturity. Sebastian concentrated on writing for the organ while at Weimar, first working extensively at studies and transcriptions from other composers to extend his vocabulary and versatility. Particularly significant was the influence of Italian composers; their simplicity and smoothness wooed Sebastian from the more strident angularity of the German tradition. With these two contrasting styles and the counterpoint characteristic of his native area, Bach

An eighteenth-century music party

evolved the music which is unmistakably his own. One result of his exposure to Italian music was a simplification of theme and treatment in his own compositions.

One of his best-known pieces of this period is his Passacaglia in C, with its orderly set of twenty variations, dividing down into two groups of ten, four sub-groups of five. But rather than ending up as a sterile, mathematical exercise, the composition exhibits rich creativity.

Also dating from about this time is Bach's *Orgel-Büchlein* ('Little Organ Book'),

In which a beginner at the organ is instructed in developing a chorale in various ways and at the same time in learning to use the pedal . . .

The book is undated, but was probably written during Sebastian's final years in Weimar. He evidently originally intended to include 164 chorales by a variety of composers, but he gave up after

49

finishing only 46. The 'Little Organ Book', written as a form of tutor, was the first of a number of such works that Sebastian was to write. In the book, he clearly abandoned the excessive complexity which so offended his Arnstadt listeners. Now his compositions were combining clarity, economy of language and great strength of emotion.

Sebastian was probably stimulated to write such a tutor by the increasing number of pupils coming to him for instruction in these years. Sebastian taught two fellow Bachs – Johann Lorenz and Johann Bernhard – as well as the Cantor Johan Tobias Krebs from the village of Buttelstädt, and J. M. Schubart, who succeeded Sebastian in his post at Weimar.

But the apparently happy course of events was not to continue. Once again Sebastian became entangled in a controversy not of his own making. A personality clash developed between the reigning Duke, Wilhelm Ernst, and his nephew and heir, Ernst August. The dictatorial Wilhelm Ernst would not tolerate the suggestions which his heir delighted in making; inevitably the rift between the two rather eccentric and self-willed aristocrats made matters particularly difficult for their employees.

The clavier player

50

Sebastian was in an especially vulnerable position. He had been teaching Ernst August the clavier, and spent a considerable amount of time at the young prince's castle, providing music, and writing and copying. When Wilhelm Ernst's patience finally broke, he prohibited his musicians from playing at his nephew's palace, despite their being joint-employees. But Sebastian's obstinacy obtruded again. He ignored the Duke's orders, and performed a birthday cantata for Ernst August, to whom he presented a birthday verse.

The furious old Duke retaliated by passing over Bach when the post of Kapellmeister fell vacant, upon the death in 1716 of old Johan Samuel Drese. Instead of his brilliant choirmaster Wilhelm Ernst eventually appointed Drese's relatively untalented son, Johann Wilhelm. It seems possible that Sebastian showed his fury by simply stopping writing new cantatas for his employer. Once again, as at Mühlhausen, Bach seems to have made no attempt to avoid or circumvent trouble; rather he seems to have become trapped into taking sides.

But in this case his friendship with Ernst August paid off. The young Duke married the sister of Prince Leopold of Anhalt-Cöthen in 1716, which gave the latter the notion of appointing Sebastian conductor at his court, upon the retirement of the previous holder of the post.

Prince Leopold, younger than Bach, was refined and musical; he sang, and played the clavier, violin and viola da gamba. But he was a Calvinist, and the Cöthen court worshipped along Reformed lines, with very simple psalm-singing the only form of liturgical music. This meant that the services expected of a court musician lay almost entirely in the secular fields; instrumental work rather than church music and organ compositions. Such a prospect represented a total about-turn for Sebastian; but a challenge rather than an obstacle. Despite this change, and the alien Reformed tradition of the Cöthen court, Bach was enthusiastic about the new possibilities offered, and accepted the young prince's invitation, settling his family at Cöthen soon after joining the prince's pay-roll in August 1717.

At this time, Sebastian became involved in a musical tournament of the kind aristocratic patrons appear to have delighted in. Travelling through Dresden, he was challenged to play the clavier in competition with the great French organist and clavier performer, Louis Marchand. But, the story runs, the contest was abortive: Marchand apparently disappeared before the event, thus admitting his inferiority to his German rival.

Despite Sebastian's happy new appointment at Cöthen, Wilhelm Ernst was unwilling to release his renowned Choirmaster. He was well aware of the brilliance of his employee – and of the fact that

Bach's new patron was related to his hated nephew. He forbade Bach to leave; but the obstinate organist 'was put under arrest for too obstinately requesting his dismissal'. He was jailed for almost a month, and when eventually released, 2 December 1717, he was given an 'unfavourable discharge'. Free to pursue his career, he departed for Cöthen. But his memory was not honoured at Weimar; the official records attempted to ignore this musician who defied his patron.

Louis Marchand (1669-1732)

Manuscript page from the *Orgelbuchlein*

Leopold of Anhalt-Cothen

6 Sadness and Joy:
Cöthen 1717-23

Sebastian now occupied a position of considerable prestige. As Court Conductor at Cöthen he received a salary of 400 thalers, which was the same as that received by the Court Marshal, the second highest court official. Prince Leopold treated Sebastian with respect and affection; the latter responded with profound compositions; he recognised that his patron 'not only loved but knew music'.

Certainly Leopold was responsible for a musical revival at court. On taking over from his widowed mother, at the age of twenty-one, the young man increased the number of court musicians from three to seventeen, so that Sebastian inherited a well-trained small orchestra on his arrival, including soloists consisting of two violins, cello, viola da gamba, oboe, bassoon and two flutes.

Cöthen

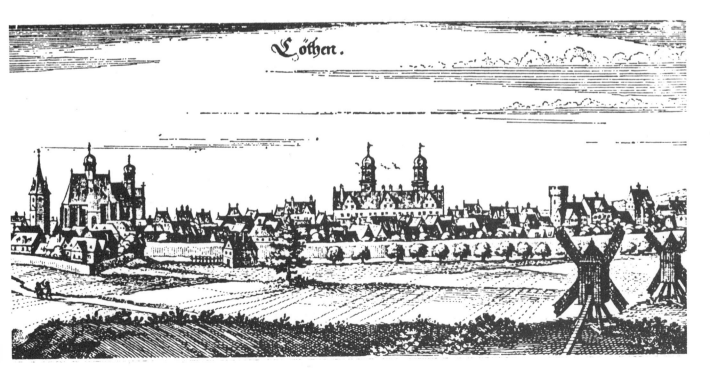

Music in an aristocrat's home in eighteenth-century Germany

Amidst such gifted performers, and stimulated by a cultivated patron. Sebastian began to produce an amazing abundance of works. Compared with the quantity of original compositions, the amount of other composers' music performed at court seems to have been minimal. Unfortunately, the great majority of his Cöthen compositions have been lost; but something of the vitality of this period is reflected in the Brandenburg Concertos, a product of these years.

There were fierce animosities between Calvinists and Lutherans in contemporary Cöthen; but by this time Sebastian seems to have learned from bitter experience not to become embroiled personally in such struggles. Though certainly never showing any tendency to switch his allegiance to the Reformed party, neither did he argue noisily for the Lutheran position. Leopold's father had permitted the building of a Lutheran church and school in Cöthen, and Sebastian was able to worship with his family and educate his children in the church of his own persuasion. For the time being, Sebastian was happy to throw all his energies into his music and his family life.

It was soon after arriving at Cöthen that Bach and Handel again came near to crossing paths. In 1719 George Frederick Handel, now settled in England, came back to Germany to find singers, and

George Frederick Handel (1685-1759)

GEORGE FREDERICK HANDEL.

Handel's harpsichord

to visit his mother in Halle, a mere twenty miles from Cöthen. As soon as he heard of Handel's presence, Sebastian rode off to Halle to try to meet him; but his great contemporary had already left on his journey back to England.

Sebastian now recognised that his eldest son, Wilhelm Friedemann, possessed a precocious musical talent, and set out to encourage the boy. We have already noticed Sebastian's 'Little Organ Book', with its provision for apprentice organists. Now he set to work on the *Clavierbüchlein vor Wilhelm Friedemann Bach*, or 'Little Clavier Book', with its ordered method of instruction for his young son.

We have a record of Sebastian's approach to teaching the clavier, reported by Philip Emanuel Bach:

The first thing he did was to teach his pupils his special ways of touching the keyboard. For this he made them practise for months nothing but separate exercises for all the fingers of both hands, with constant attention to the production of a clean clear tone. Over a period of some months, no pupil was excused these exercises, and, according to his firm opinion, they should be continued from six to twelve months at least. But if he found that anyone, after some months of practice began to lose patience, he was so considerate as to write little pieces in which these exercises were linked together. To this type belong the 'Six Little Preludes for Beginners', and still more the fifteen 'Two-Part Inventions'. He wrote both down during his teaching, and so attended to the immediate needs of the pupil; afterwards he transformed these pieces into beautiful, expressive little works of art . . . After this he set his pupils to studying his own greater compositions which, as he well knew, would give them the best means of exercising their powers.

Carl Philipp Emanuel tells how his father was similarly ordered in teaching his pupils composition. He only took on pupils he

TITLE PAGE [24]

Little Clavier Book
for
Wilhelm Friedemann Bach
begun in Cöthen
on January 22
Anno 1720

The title page of Bach's 'Little Clavier Book for Wilhelm Friedemann Bach, begun in Cöthen on January 22 Anno 1720'

considered gifted and imaginative; and having taken them on, they were put through a stiff course. They began 'studies by learning pure four-part thorough bass. From this he went on to chorales; first he added the basses to them himself, then he taught them to devise the basses themselves . . .'

The *Clavierbüchlein* starts off by explaining the musical clefs, and then takes the beginner through from the most elementary pieces to considerably more complex compositions. Among the pieces in the book, probably the more important are the two-part and three-part inventions, perfect little examples of musical structure, combining technical virtuosity and emotional depth.

But Sebastian's life was not all joy, even at Cöthen. In May 1720 he travelled with his patron, Leopold, to take the waters at Carlsbad. When he returned to Cöthen in July he found that his wife Maria Barbara had died during his absence. We know very little about her, but everything seems to indicate that they had a contented family life. Sebastian was now left with four children to look after: Catherina Dorothea, Wilhelm Friedemann, Carl Philipp Emanuel and Johann Gottfried.

St Catherine's Church, Hamburg

This blow abruptly brought Sebastian back to his thoughts of death – the release of the body. He suddenly realised that, for all his enjoyment of freedom at Cöthen, he still needed to express his deeply-rooted faith by writing church music. Hence his interest in an invitation from the authorities of St James' Church, Hamburg, to compete for the position of organist in the same year. Sebastian travelled to Hamburg, but was unable to play his trial performance on the day required, since he was due back in Cöthen. But he did play on the organ of the now very aged Reinken at St Catherine's, winning the gratifying – and rarely awarded – praise of the old master: 'I thought this art [improvising on a chorale] was dead; but I see it lives in you.'

It is not entirely clear why Bach did not take up the post in Hamburg; the Council seems to have favoured his appointment, but Sebastian was apparently outraged by the suggestion that the successful candidate should pay for the privilege of obtaining the office. (It was still a custom in Hamburg for certain positions to be purchased.)

Some years later Johann Matheson gave an embellished version of the incident, mentioning no names, but clearly referring to Bach and Hamburg:

I remember, and a whole large congregation will probably also remember, that a few years ago a certain great virtuoso, whose abilities have since brought him a handsome Cantorship, presented himself as candidate for the post of organist in a town of no small size, displayed his playing on the most various and greatest organs, and aroused universal admiration for his ability; but there presented himself at the same time . . . the son of a well-to-do artisan, who was better at preluding with his thalers than with his fingers, and he obtained the post . . . despite the fact that almost everyone was angry about it. This took place at Christmas, and the eloquent chief preacher, who had not concurred in the deliberations, expounded splendidly the gospel of the music of the angels at the birth of Christ, in which connection the recent incident of the rejected artist gave him quite naturally the opportunity to reveal his thoughts, and to close his sermon with something like the following: he was firmly convinced that even if one of the angels of Bethlehem should come down from Heaven, one who played divinely and wished to become organist of St James', but had no means, he might just as well fly away again.

But Sebastian seems not to have taken such events too hard; he was busy meanwhile on new compositions. In March 1721 he completed careful copies of six of his orchestral concertos. They were dedicated to Christian Ludwig, Margrave of Brandenburg, who evidently commissioned them two years earlier, probably after meeting Sebastian at Carlsbad. In fact the concertos had been played previously by the Cöthen orchestra – and it appears that the

Margrave had insufficient musical resources to perform the music himself, at least as scored by Bach.

These are, of course, the pieces we now know as the 'Brandenburg Concertos'. Sebastian had no opportunity to write concertos before coming to Cöthen; he now entered into this new possibility with enthusiasm. Sebastian generally favoured the form of concerto written by Vivaldi, with three movements: fast, slow, and then fast, though clarifying and simplifying the Italian's

61

approach. Two violin concertos and a concerto for two violins and orchestra also survive from among his compositions at Cöthen.

The Brandenburg Concertos are not written for a single solo instrument, but for several wind instruments, in a more old-fashioned style. In the first, third and sixth Brandenburgs, the orchestra is evenly-divided, and each section answers the other to give an overall balance. The second, fourth and fifth concertos feature a small group of solo instruments accompanied by the orchestra. In the second, for instance, the small group, or 'concertino', consists of violin, oboe, recorder and trumpet; in the fifth, of flute, violin and harpsichord, although it is the keyboard instrument which is consistently in the limelight. In effect, this is among the finest concertos in history to be written for the keyboard. Probably Sebastian himself was the first player of the harpsichord part.

But over and above the techniques and the orchestration, the Brandenburg Concertos are brimming with joy and brilliance; effervescent and alert, their rhythm and colour reflect the assurance and delight of life at the Cöthen court. Sebastian seems to have responded with enthusiasm to the chance to write music for a group of accomplished musicians.

At this time, too, Sebastian wrote two Orchestral Suites – one in B minor for the flute, consisting of an overture and a set of exuberant dances, culminating in the delightful, light-spirited *Badinerie*; and the other for two oboes, bassoon and strings.

It was while at Cöthen, too, that Sebastian completed work on the first set of twenty-four preludes and fugues, which were to make up the first volume of his *Das Wohltemperierte Clavier* ('The Well-tempered Clavier') or 'Preludes and Fugues through all the tones and semitones . . . for the use and profit of young musicians anxious to learn as well as for the amusement of those already skilled in this art . . .' In other words, he wrote one prelude and fugue for each key, major and minor. They were so popular that Sebastian was later prompted to write a second set of twenty-four; hence the well-known 'Forty-Eight', which has established Bach ever since as a master of keyboard composition, and the master of fugue.

The unusual title, the 'well-tempered clavier', comes from the contemporary discovery that by replacing the pure, mathematical tuning of a keyboard instrument with a slightly 'impure' tuning, any note could be taken for the tonic, with no need for subsequent re-tuning. This seems to have stimulated Sebastian to explore thoroughly every possibility of the 'well-tempered' keyboard. But the 'Twenty-Four', though written as a set, display a remarkable variety within the constraints observed.

With four motherless children, it was clearly imperative for

Johann Sebastian Bach in 1720

Manuscript of the beginning of the first movement of the sixth Brandenburg concerto due Viole da Gamba, Violoncello, Violone è Cembalo.

Christian Ludwig,
Margrave of Brandenburg

The castle of Cothen

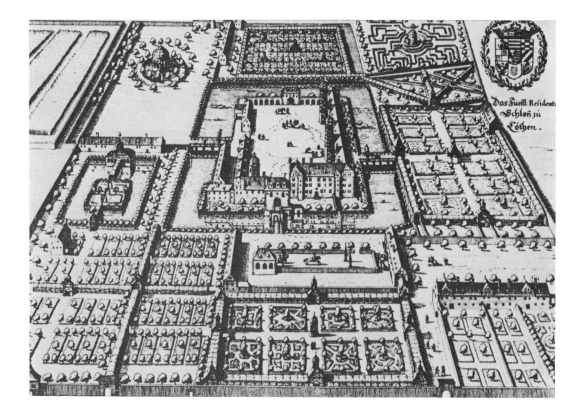

Part of Bach's manuscript for 'The Well-Tempered Clavier' (Fugue XI, Vol I)

Sebastian to re-marry. Despite the habit in the Bach family of finding a new wife rapidly, Sebastian waited eighteen months before his second marriage. This time his choice fell upon Anna Magdalena Wilcken, daughter of the Court Trumpeter of the Prince of Saxe-Weissenfels, and descended on both sides from a musical family. Anna Magdalena was herself a singer, and earned a salary half that of Sebastian's at the Cöthen court. The Castle Church register records that they were married at Bach's home on 3 December 1721, when Anna Magdalena was still only twenty – Sebastian was now thirty-six. We know a little more of Anna Magdalena than of Maria Barbara; Sebastian seems to have been truly devoted to her, and their common expertise as musicians must have drawn them closer together.

Anna Magdalena was to bear thirteen children, although seven of them died as infants. A moving reflection of their intimacy is revealed in the two notebooks which the couple compiled together. The first, the *Clavierbüchlein* ('Little Clavier Book for Anna Magdalena') was collected together in 1722. Most of the works in this book were probably written as technical exercises, or to entertain the family, although it also includes five French suites.

63

A young harpsichordist and flautist

The second notebook, much longer, was finished in 1725, and is more revealing. There is a delightfully touching poem in it, conceivably by Bach, but certainly reflecting his outlook, pointing out in a homely, lighthearted way some similarities between a man and his pipe:

> Whene'er I take my pipe and stuff it
> And smoke to pass the time away,
> My thoughts, as I sit then and puff it,
> Dwell on a picture sad and grey.
> It teaches me that very like
> Am I myself unto my pipe.

Like me, this pipe so fragrant burning
  Is made of naught but earth and clay;
To earth I too shall be returning,
  It falls and, ere I'd think to say,
  It breaks in two before my eyes;
  In store for me a like fate lies.

No stain the pipe's hue yet doth darken;
  It remains white. Thus do I know
That when to death's call I must hearken
  My body, too, all pale will grow.
  To black beneath the sod 'twill turn,
  Likewise, the pipe, if oft it burn.

Or when the pipe is fairly glowing,
  Behold then instantaneously,
The smoke off into thin air going,
  Till naught but ash is left to see.
  Man's frame likewise away will burn
  And unto dust his body turn.

How oft it happens when one's smoking:
  The stopper's missing from its shelf,
And one goes with one's finger poking
  Into the bowl and burns oneself.
  If in the pipe such pain doth dwell,
  How hot must be the pains of Hell.

Thus o'er my pipe, in contemplation
  Of such things, I can constantly
Indulge in fruitful meditation,
  And so, puffing contentedly,
  On land, on sea, at home, abroad,
  I smoke my pipe and worship God.

Sebastian also wrote a song expressing his love for his young wife:

If thou be near, I go rejoicing
To peace and rest beyond the skies,
Nor will I fear what may befall me,
For I will hear thy sweet voice call me,
Thy gentle hand will close my eyes.

For Bach, there was no incongruity in linking love and death. In the same little note-book, Sebastian also wrote three different versions

Pan pedibus plaudunt choreas. Kp VI X.

A French dancer at the
time of Louis XIV

of his tune to Paul Gerhardt's hymn 'Fear not, my soul, on God rely . . .', obviously directing this favourite piece to his wife.

Not only does the book include Sebastian's additions, but also pages filled with Anna Magdalena's little dances – marches, polonaises, and minuets – possibly written for their young children to play. Such pieces were also admirably suited to dancing, and their sons and daughters could well have used them for the traditional dancing lessons. The books also include Sebastian's French Suites and English Suites – collections of dances for keyboard.

But another marriage brought an end to the happy period at Cöthen. A week after the Bach wedding, Prince Leopold married his cousin, Friederica Henrietta, daughter to Prince Carl-Friedrich of Anhalt-Bernberg. Suddenly the musical life of the court was threatened, since the young princess seems to have been totally devoid of musical interests or appreciation. She may have found Leopold's affection for his Court Conductor too great a threat to her own relationship; certainly music ceased to play a central role at the Cöthen court, and Sebastian began to feel rather superfluous. Possibly he was again feeling that he would like to work in a church context, and considering how best to further his sons' education. Certainly he began to prepare himself for another move.

Frederica Henrietta of Anhalt-Cothen

Title page of "The Well-Tempered Clavier"

7 The Call to Leipzig: 1723-26

5 June 1722 Johann Kuhnau, for the previous twenty-one years the Leipzig Thomas Cantor, died. When the Town Council came to discuss his successor, their first choice fell upon Georg Philipp Telemann, recently appointed Music Director and Cantor of Hamburg, after having held the post of organist at the New Church in Leipzig. The citizens of Leipzig were extraordinarily

Leipzig in 1632

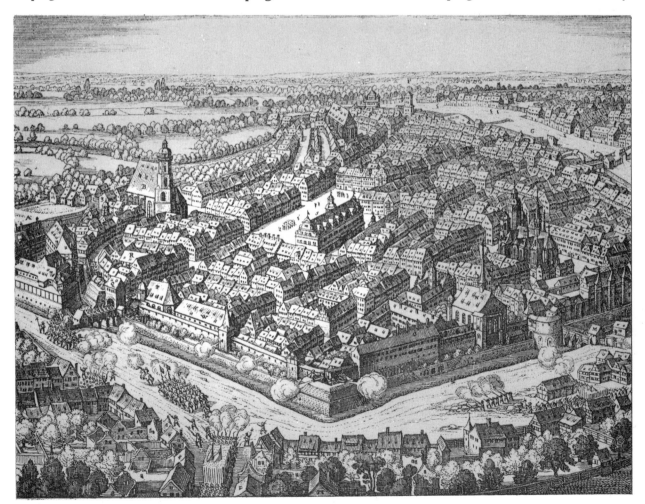

1. Die St Thomas Kirche. 2. Die Thomas Schule.
3. Der Steinerne Wasser=Kasten

Krüger fe Liplia.

Die Thomaskirche und Thomasschule in Leipzig zur Zeit Bachs.
Nach einem Stich von Krüger (1723).
Aus Leipzig durch drei Jahrhunderte von Dr. G. Wustmann.

68

enthusiastic to get hold of Telemann; he took advantage of this to
stipulate that, if appointed, he should undertake no non-musical
duties at the school of St Thomas. However, once the invitation had
been extended to him, he used this as a bargaining counter to
extract a rise in his salary in Hamburg, leaving Leipzig still without
a Thomas Cantor. Sebastian had not previously applied, since
Telemann was a personal friend.

Sebastian did now apply, along with four other candidates,
including the Court Musician of Darmstadt, Christoph Graupner,
an ex-pupil of the school of St Thomas. In the event, it was
Graupner who was selected; but matters conspired to prevent his
taking the post. His patron, the Landgrave, would not let him go,
and put up his salary to satisfy the disappointed musician. When
Graupner had to pull out in May 1723, he supported Sebastian's
candidature.

The post of Thomas Cantor at Leipzig was influential in the
extreme. The Cantor was in effect musical director of the city's
churches – a city where Lutheranism was a vigorous, lively
movement. For centuries, the choir school of St Thomas provided
singers for the services at St Thomas', and a succession of
renowned cantors had held the post. But the Cantor was in a
difficult position. He was subject to the authority of the Rector of
the school; to the City Council, made up of three burgomasters, two
deputy burgomasters and ten assessors; and to the Church
Consistory, who supervised the church services – both theologically
and musically. To find himself answerable to these determined
authorities after his relatively untroubled years at Cöthen was a
problem for Bach. Moreover he had enjoyed considerable social
prestige as Court Conductor for Prince Leopold, a role which
would diminish with his possible move to Leipzig.

Even financially he was not sure of improving his status at
Leipzig; the basic salary was not even a quarter of what the Prince
paid him; he would have to rely on fees from weddings, funerals,
teaching and other duties to supplement this. Anna Magdalena's
role would change even more drastically: an accomplished soprano
soloist for Prince Leopold, she could expect to have no
opportunities for regular performances in Leipzig, since women
were prohibited from church solo work.

In the end, two factors seem to have persuaded a probably
somewhat reluctant Sebastian to try to make the change. Leipzig,
with the school of St Thomas and its illustrious university, opened
up the prospect of a fine education for his sons; and he also seems to
have built up a yearning to create church music again. In the period
of indecision, with the Cöthen atmosphere unsympathetic to his
musical activities, he was working on the *St John Passion*, ready for
its first performance soon after his arrival in Leipzig.

In fact, Sebastian performed a trial in Leipzig as early as 7 February 1723. He played his own cantata, *Jesus nahm zu sich die Zwölfe* ('Jesus called to him the Twelve'), probably singing the bass part himself. With Graupner's failure to take up the position, Sebastian determined to apply. The Leipzig authorities similarly now determined to secure his services. But only in the attitude of 'if we can't have the best, we must make do with what there is', as a Leipzig Councillor voiced it. Undoubtedly, Sebastian's virtuosity at the organ was now known throughout Germany; but the Thomas Cantor was not required to play the organ. It is unlikely that the Leipzig Council knew of his outpouring of music, since scarcely any of his compositions had yet been printed. Moreover, though his position as Court Conductor was socially elevated, it did not rank in weight with the positions of his rivals, Telemann and Graupner. The Leipzig Council also frowned on Sebastian's lack of formal education; however formidable a musician he might be, he could make no great claim to academic virtuosity.

To avoid yet another disappointment, Leipzig asked Sebastian to obtain a letter of dismissal before proceeding to his election. Leopold was clearly sorry to see his friend and employee depart; but he put no obstacles in his way. Rather did he provide a generous letter of dismissal in the form of a testimonial:

We have had in our service and under our patronage the respectable and learned Johann Sebastian Bach, since 5 August 1717, as conductor and Director of our Chamber Music. We have at all times been very satisfied with his execution of his duties, but the said Bach, wishing now to seek his fortune elsewhere, has humbly petitioned us to grant him a most gracious dismissal . . .

Equipped with this release, Sebastian sent off his application, with his agreement to the terms of the Council, except for a request to appoint an assistant to give Latin lessons for him. Now at last the election went ahead, but the time taken to secure a new Cantor, and the caveats entered by various councillors, all pointed to the troubles that Sebastian had in store. One councillor asked that his church music should not be 'too theatrical' – another ominous note.

Bach proceeded to sign various documents, including an agreement not to leave the city without permission from the Burgomaster, and, after successfully negotiating a theological test, he was ready to take up his new post, 30 May 1723. Before the Bach family left Cöthen, Prince Leopold's young wife died. This could have swayed Bach against leaving; but his mind was made up. Although he was not persuaded to stay, he remained on the friendliest of terms with his one-time patron.

Sebastian continued to return to Cöthen periodically to make

71

'Morning prayers with Bach' (T. E. Rosenthal)

music, and when Leopold re-married two years later, Sebastian wrote a cantata to mark his second wife's birthday. But Leopold died suddenly in November 1728, and with him the brief flowering of music at the Cöthen court. In March 1729 Sebastian travelled to Cöthen for the last time, to conduct a special funeral cantata based on the *St Matthew Passion*, which had not yet received a public performance.

When Sebastian came to Leipzig, four children accompanied him: Catherina Dorothea (15), Wilhelm Friedemann (13), Carl Philipp Emanuel (9) and Gottfried Bernhard (8). The boys all studied as pupils at the School of St Thomas, and also joined the choir, studying the organ, clavier and musical theory.

Sebastian was formally installed as Cantor on 1 June 1723. He found the school in a appalling state. It was outdated and overcrowded. Its Rector, Johann Heinrich Ernesti, was seventy-one, and totally incapable of disciplining pupils or teachers. The pupils were made up of paying day-boys, and roughly fifty Foundation Scholars, most of whom were boarding for a nominal fee, accepted on account of their musical ability. These boys were mainly from poor, deprived backgrounds, and needed firm discipline; this Ernesti totally failed to provide.

Johann Heinrich Ernesti

Bach's contract with the city of Leipzig

[Handwritten contract text in German cursive script, dated "den 5. Maii, 1723", signed] Johann Sebastian Bach.

Johann Kuhnau (1660-1722)

Title page of the *Clavierbuchlein* ("Little Clavier Book for Anna Magdalena Bach"

The physical arrangements at the school were completely inadequate. There were insufficient beds to accommodate all the boarders; a single classroom was called upon to house three classes simultaneously, and to be the dining-room. The boys were subject to disease and sickness. They were overworked, and were forced to sing at funerals, whatever the weather. Worse still, they sang daily in the city streets during the first half of January each year, to attract charitable gifts. Not surprisingly, packed closely in insanitary conditions, the boys were prone to a succession of diseases and ailments. Most of the choirboys were between thirteen and sixteen when they first arrived at the school, although sometimes considerably older.

The school routine was rigorous, and Sebastian himself was closely bound by it:

The bell rings at 5am in summer and 6am in winter, when every scholar rises, washes, brushes his hair, and is ready . . . to attend prayers, bringing his Bible with him.

Once every four weeks Sebastian, as Cantor, had to act as inspector, conducting prayers in the morning and evening, supervising discipline, calling the roll, and going to see any pupils isolated in the sanatorium on account of illness.

Sebastian rehearsed the senior boys on Monday, Tuesday, Wednesday and Friday mornings, and on Friday took the boys to the early morning service. Saturday found the Cantor teaching

Bach's house, Leipzig

73

Luther's Catechism, and practising the cantata for the following day's service, which went on from seven in the morning until midday. The cantata which Bach provided was normally based on the text of the Gospel or Epistle for the day.

Sebastian and his family had to live in the midst of this chaos. They had rooms in a part of the school buildings, and, although there was a separate entrance, Sebastian's study was divided from the sixth-form room by only a plaster divide.

But Sebastian always saw himself as primarily Director of Music. This stored up trouble for him with the Leipzig authorities, who expected him also to fulfil his duties as teacher and choirmaster adequately. As Director of Music, he had overall responsibility for music in all of the Leipzig churches, particularly St Thomas' and St Nicholas', with their long and elaborate Sunday services.

Sebastian was particularly enthusiastic about the musical arrangements at St Thomas'. The church had been renovated and the organ reconstructed; and the church building was claimed to be 'one of the most elaborate and beautiful places of worship in existence . . . adorned with an exquisite and costly altar'. There were conveniently-sited wooden galleries on either side of the organ, where Sebastian could deploy his instrumentalists, while the choir was placed in front of the organ. An additional miniature organ, sited high in the altar-wall could be used by Sebastian for special high-register effects. Although St Nicholas' Church had a more powerful organ, which Sebastian preferred as a solo instrument, the other arrangements there did not rival those at St Thomas'.

In his first years in Leipzig, the new Cantor worked ceaselessly to provide the church music required. He apparently completed a total of five sets of cantatas for the church year, which would amount in all to 295 cantatas, although considerably fewer than this have actually survived. This figure averages out at something like one new cantata per month between arriving at Leipzig and 1744. In addition, he was engaged in writing motets for the more important city funerals, and civic music, as well as a Passion for Good Friday.

In April 1724 came the first performance of the *St John Passion*. Although, for reasons outlined above, Bach would have preferred this to take place at St Thomas', the City Council insisted that the policy of Passion music being performed in alternate years at St Nicholas' and St Thomas' be adhered to. Sebastian complied, but:

pointed out that the booklet (libretto) was already printed, that there was no room available, and that the harpsichord needed repair, all of which, however, could be attended to at little cost; but he requested at any rate that a little additional room be provided in the choir-loft, so that he could

The manuscript of the
first page of the *St John
Passion*

place the people needed for the music, and that the harpsichord be
repaired.

The response of the Council was that:

The Cantor should . . . have a notice printed stating that the music was to
take place this time in St Nicholas' Church, have the necessary
arrangements made in the choir loft, with the help of the sexton, and get
the harpsichord repaired.

The idea of chanting the story of the Passion in Holy Week dated back centuries earlier to a time when the Gospel for the day was intoned by the priest, to carry it through the entire church building. Most of the text of Bach's *St John Passion* was taken from the Bible – particularly of course from St John's Gospel. The Evangelist carries forward the narrative, in the form of a recitative; the parts of the main characters are sung by soloists, the crowd scenes by the chorus. Arias are sung between the narrative, to express the way in which the individual believer responds to the events; and chorales, sung by the whole congregation, fulfil the same function. The composer himself conducted the *St John Passion* four times, and made modifications at subsequent performances.

We have previously noticed the way that Bach tended to react against Pietism, because of his strongly orthodox training. In

A selection of eighteenth-century musical instruments

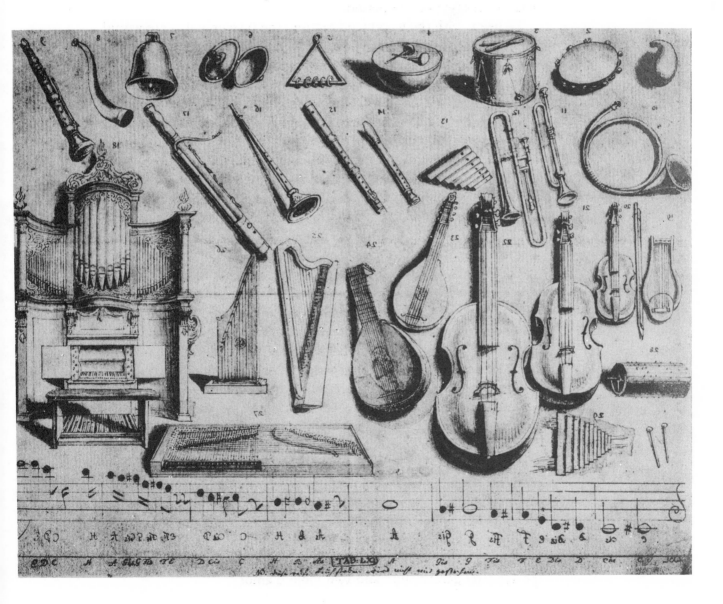

Leipzig, Pietism had a strong influence, especially since Halle, a centre of this mystical, intense movement, was only a few miles distant. There is certainly evidence that the texts of Bach's passion music reflect both orthodox and Pietist sentiments.

What were the instrumental forces on which Sebastian could call for the performance of his Passions? Since there was no princely court, Leipzig had no court orchestra. As an Imperial Free City, Leipzig had only its town musicians, who were joined by non-professionals to make up the church musicians. The town musicians were called upon to make music at both church and city events. We will discover later what Sebastian thought of the standard of performance of some of the Leipzig instrumentalists. Even the instruments they used were different in sound from those we know today. For this very reason, there is a modern fashion to attempt to play eighteenth-century music on authentic instruments, and in the style of the period.

To begin with the woodwind section, the instruments here would have been much simpler, with fewer keys than their modern equivalents. This meant that it was much more difficult to get accurate notes, particularly in some of the more complex keys. Bach frequently scored his music for the recorder as well as the flute, while the oboe was probably considerably louder, more raucous, and especially difficult for the player trying to hit his notes accurately. As well as the family of oboes – the oboe d'amore, oboe da caccia and oboe taille – Sebastian also scored for the bassoon. He used brass instruments fully, particularly the trumpet – though they were not employed for Passion music, since according to the 'Doctrine of Affections' this would have been counter to the spirit of the material.

The strings of Bach's time – violin, viola and cello – were less strong than their modern descendants. They had lower bridges, all gut strings and were played with a shorter, lighter bow, giving a softer, rougher note, but being very adaptable to light dance music. Instead of our double-bass, Bach scored for the violone, which played at the same pitch as the modern bass, but more quietly. Bach also scored for a kettledrum section in his orchestra.

Singing styles, too, contrasted with those of today. Probably soloists had a small vibrato to their note, which would have lent an operatic effect to their performance of cantatas or Passions. Similarly, the choristers would not have the fine purity we associate with the English cathedral tradition, but a more resonant, full-throated sound.

For the *St John Passion*, then, Sebastian scored for a normal-strength Passion orchestra: two flutes, two oboes, bassoon, strings and continuo. He also included parts for obsolescent instruments: the viola da gamba, lute and two viole d'amore.

Bach's organ at the Thomaskirche

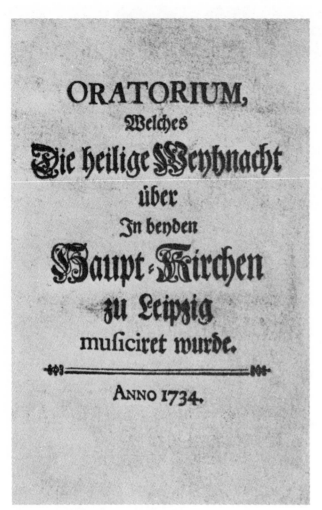

ORATORIUM,
Welches
Die heilige Weyhnacht
über
In beyden
Haupt-Kirchen
zu Leipzig
musiciret wurde.
—⚹—————⚹—
ANNO 1734.

Title page of the *Christmas Oratorio*

Am 1sten Heil. Weyhnacht-
Feyertage,
Frühe zu St. Nicolai und Nachmit-
tage zu St. Thomæ.

Tutti.

Jauchzet! frohlocket! auf! preiset
die Tage,
Rühmet, was heute der Höchste ge-
than,
Lasset das Zagen, verbannet die Klage,
Stimmet voll Jauchzen und Frö-
lichkeit an:
Dienet dem Höchsten mit herrlichen
Chören
Laßt uns den Nahmen des Höchsten
verehren.

Da Capo.

A 2   Evan-

First page of the text of the *Christmas Oratorio*

The cantatas which Sebastian wrote while at Leipzig encompass an amazing variety of moods: texts cover anything from strict Lutheran orthodoxy to the more uninhibited Pietist emotions. Similarly, musically, there is a coming together of a wide range of new and older styles. Bach's settings match the texts: brilliant, illustrative, profound, symbolic, intense. Sebastian may well have been responsible for his own libretti in some instances, though, Picander (Friedrich Henrici) was often his writer.

In addition to the great body of cantatas, Sebastian wrote six motets, using similar texts to those in his early cantatas; they were derived from chorales and from the Bible. In the 1730s, Sebastian wrote three works he labelled 'oratorio'. The most important of these was his *Christmas Oratorio,* a series of six cantatas performed around Christmas. Like the passions, New Testament passages are sung by the Evangelist, as narrator, individual's speech is conveyed by a soloist, and group sayings by the choir. Chorales and arias are interspersed throughout.

Sebastian's *Magnificat* was originally written in 1723 for Christmas performance, but in 1730 it was revised, transposed, re-orchestrated and shortened. It is among the most compact and joyous of his works.

8 Troubles in Leipzig: 1727-30

Before very long, the difficulties of having a multiplicity of authorities to answer to in Leipzig began to raise real problems for Sebastian. The first real controversy arose in his relations with the University Church of St Paul's. Until 1710, there had been only a limited number of services held there, at special feast-days and university occasions; for this so-called 'Old Service' the Thomas Cantor was traditionally responsible. But in 1710, the university introduced a weekly Sunday 'New Service', of which Bach's predecessor, Kuhnàu, only obtained musical direction with considerable difficulty. Upon his death, a previous organist at St Paul's, J G Görner, cleverly intervened, and offered his services freely, depriving Bach of the directorship of the New Service when he was in turn appointed Thomas Cantor.

Sebastian was seriously put out: he wanted both the fees emanating from this additional appointment, and the close links with the university which it afforded. He first attempted to stake his claim by performing his duties at the 'Old Service' with his customary virtuosity; but the university was not impressed enough to give him the full amount paid to the previous Thomas Cantor. They held back fourteen thalers, which led the deprived Sebastian in 1725 to write a series of three letters to the highest arbitration: the Elector of Saxony, Augustus. His petitioning did achieve something; he was awarded the missing money, but the university was still unwilling to grant him both 'Old' and 'New' Services. Having failed to secure his rights, Sebastian now took what we may recognise as characteristic action: he lost all interest in St Paul's, and got one of his pupils to carry out his duties as musical director for the 'Old Service'. But the university in its turn retaliated; they had always showed their contempt for the new Thomas Cantor's lack of academic training. With this additional grievance, they pettily made sure that special musical commissions were placed elsewhere whenever possible, thus depriving Sebastian of the fees

St Nicholas' Church,
Leipzig

which he needed to make up his income.

Further problems ensued shortly illustrating the chequered path of Sebastian's career at this point. In 1727, Hans Carl von Kirchbach, an aristocratic university student, volunteered to pay for a special commemmorative service at St Paul's, to mark the death of Christiane Eberhardine, the faithful Lutheran wife of the Elector of Saxony. He received permission, and commissioned a funeral ode from the poet Johann Christoph Gottsched, to be set by Bach. At this point the querulous university authorities objected that Görner was the right man to compose such music. When Kirchbach in turn objected that the music was already written, he was informed that Görner, not Bach, was to perform it. Kirchbach

Leipzig from the fields

was insistent; thereupon the university stipulated that Görner could be paid off with a twelve-thaler sweetener, while the Thomas Cantor was required to sign a statement that he would not make any more arrangements for music for St Paul's without first getting their consent. This was to try Sebastian's patience too far; the man dispatched to obtain his signature was summarily ejected.

But while the hidebound officials spurned the brilliant musician in their midst, the students of Leipzig drew closer to this virtuoso, stimulating him to produce several of his secular cantatas. Not only so, but he attracted a number of university students to participate in his music. For instance, one of the law students, CG Wecker, was such an asset musically that Sebastian cited this in his favour when, in March 1729, Wecker applied for the post of Cantor at Schweidnitz:

82

His knowledge in musical matters has made him a welcome guest everywhere, particularly since he has a good command of various instruments and no less can well afford to make himself heard vocally, and has also been able to give creditable assistance in my church and other music . . .

G F Handel conducting an oratorio

A similar relationship of master and student obviously developed later with Bernhard Dieterich Ludewig, for whom Sebastian provided the following touching testimonial in 1737:

... he has not only done well in his theological studies, but also for several years frequented my *Collegium musicum* with diligence, taking part tirelessly in it, playing various instruments as well as singing on many occasions, and has generally so distinguished himself that I have found myself able to entrust the younger members of my family to his careful teaching, and also taught him regularly myself in those areas of music with which he was as yet unfamiliar.

But further difficulties arose in the musical life of the churches. By tradition, the Cantor had the right to choose the hymns sung at Vespers. When this privilege was challenged in 1728 by a sub-deacon at St Nicholas', who selected his own hymns, Sebastian objected. He petitioned the Leipzig church authorities, the Consistory, but they came out on the side of their minister, telling Bach to accept his choice:

When the ministers who are preaching have it announced that particular hymns are to be sung before or after the sermon, he shall be ruled accordingly, and have the same sung.

Sebastian next took the issue up with the Leipzig City Council, but although they eventually found in his favour, this was on the basis of pragmatism rather than precedent. As Sebastian mentioned in his own letter to the Council:

When, in addition to the music for voices and instruments, very long hymns are sung, the divine service is held up, and all sorts of disorder would have to be reckoned with.

Since in fact some of the hymns were more than thirty verses in length, the Consistory eventually saw some point in restricting their use. When the *Leipzig Song Book* was published in 1729, it was stipulated that for the future all hymns were to be selected from this collection.

In the meantime, Sebastian had to continue with his regular duties, which included providing music for non-ecclesiastical events. He wrote a special secular cantata to mark the birthday of Augustus II in 1727, and this was performed on 12 May by the Foundation Pupils at St Thomas'.

The chief copy of the aria, which was to be presented to His Majesty, the Foundation Scholars had bound in scarlet velvet, with gilt tassels and gold fringes, printed on white satin, and it was carried by the orator . . . upon a silver plate.

The procession was arranged as follows:

1 The senior students of the fifteen tables in the refectory, together with a sixteenth, with wax torches.

Frederick Augustus II,
Elector of Saxony

84

2 Two marshals with batons.

3 The Orator . . . accompanied by two others.

4 The table companions of four tables, with burning torches.

5 The Chorus Musicus, who played trumpets and kettledrums and other instruments on the march.

6 The rest of the Foundation Students with torches . . . Everything had been prepared for the music, which was then performed to his Majesty's pleasure, in the presence of a great gathering of people.

But all this was a lead-up to the performance of Sebastian's most ambitious work until this point in his career. On Good Friday (15 April) 1729 came the first performance of his *St Matthew Passion* at St Thomas'. He had been at work on this massive enterprise for some time, and had adapted suitable parts of it for use at Prince Leopold's interment at Cöthen in the earlier part of the year.

The text for the *St Matthew Passion* was supplied by the Leipzig Postal Commissioner, C F Henrici, under his normal pseudonym of Picander. Its considerable size required many accomplished musicians; presumably Bach made good use of talented university students as well as other capable performers, such as older members of his own family. For a subsequent performance, we know that Sebastian used two orchestras each of seventeen instrumentalists,

St Thomas' Church, Leipzig

two twelve-voice choruses, and for the chorales a twelve-voice choir.

Although massive and lengthy, lasting more than three hours, the Passion was written to fit within the normal Good Friday pattern of services. This traditionally was as follows:

1.15pm Church bells tolled
Hymn: *Da Jesu an dem Kreuze* sung by choir
Passion Music, Part I
Versicle: *Herr Jesus Christ, dich zu uns wend*
Sermon
Passion Music, Part II
Motet, *Ecce quomodo moritur*
Passion Versicle
Collection
Hymn: *Nun danket alle Gott*

The *St Matthew Passion* is often seen as the culmination of Sebastian's writing for the church. Whereas the *St John Passion* displays a certain violence and even anger, the *St Matthew* is gentler and much more intimate, with a moving combination of joy and grief. The sayings of Christ are recitatives accompanied only by the organ in the *St John Passion;* in the *St Matthew* the soloist is joined by a string quartet, who only desist in the agonized cry of 'My God, why hast Thou forsaken me?'

Sebastian enjoyed the opportunity to experiment with his settings for both voices and instruments. In the *St John Passion,* he frequently repeated the music for the crowd to contribute to the architectural balance of the whole structure. By contrast, the choruses of the *St Matthew Passion* are of amazing variety, each peculiarly suited to the text set. On the other hand, Sebastian repeats the chorales throughout the work – particularly 'Oh Sacred Head Now Wounded' – but with different words and harmonies as the context dictates. The most elaborate piece of writing is the chorale melody serving as a *cantus firmus,* performed in the early occasions by the organist, but sung at later performances by a boys' choir.

Despite the towering achievement of this work, we have no record of the reception of its first performance in Leipzig. It must have caused something of a sensation, knowing what we do of the conservatism of the Leipzig authorities. There was in all likelihood a noticeable coolness towards the innovatory parts of the new Passion.

Whatever its reception, Sebastian's trials with the authorities continued. The next May he was asked to fill the nine vacant places for Foundation Scholars at St Thomas'. He made trials of twenty-three applicants, and wrote a very careful report on their musical proficiency. Eleven he rejected outright as totally without merit;

the others he listed, with a note as to their voice and musical training: 'has a good strong voice and fine proficiency'; 'voice somewhat weak and proficiency indifferent' and so forth. Apparently deliberately snubbing their Cantor, the City Council appointed four Foundationers whom Sebastian had dismissed, a fifth whom he had not even auditioned, and only accepted five of those he had seen fit to recommend.

The rift continued to widen. The following year, matters had deteriorated enough for the Leipzig City Council to debate Bach's behaviour. They claimed that:

he had not conducted himself as he should (without telling the Burgomaster in office he sent a choir student to the country; went away without asking leave) for which he must be reproached and admonished . . . Not only did the Cantor do nothing, but he was not even willing to offer an explanation of why this was so; he did not hold the singing class.

As a result of this dissatisfaction, and with the feeling that Bach was incorrigible, a motion was passed to cut down the Cantor's income by restricting his fees for occasional duties.

This dispute was certainly not one-sided. Sebastian, for his part, was exasperated by the conditions under which he was expected to work. Provoked beyond bearing, he penned a lengthy statement of his feelings about church music in Leipzig, submitting it to the Council, 23 August 1730:

A short, but indispensable sketch of what constitutes well-appointed church music, with a few impartial reflections on its present state of decline.

For well-appointed church music, singers and instrumentalists are necessary. In this town the singers are provided by the Foundation Pupils of St Thomas', and are in four sections: trebles, altos, tenors and basses. If the choirs are to perform church music properly . . . the singers must be sub-divided into two groups for the solos and for the chorus. There are usually four of the former, but sometimes up to eight if it is desired to perform music for two choirs. There must be at least eight of the latter group, two to each part . . .

The number of resident pupils at St Thomas' is fifty-five; these are divided into four choirs, for the four churches in which they partly perform music for voices and instruments, partly sing motets, and partly chorales. For three of the churches, namely St Thomas', St Nicholas' and the New Church, all the pupils must be musically trained . . . those who can only sing a chorale when needed go to St Peter's.

In each choir there must be at least three trebles, three altos, three tenors and the same number of basses, so that if one is unable to sing (which often happens, particularly at this time of year, as is shown by the doctor's prescriptions sent to the dispensary) a motet can still be sung with at least two voices to each part . . .

Manuscript page from *St. Matthew Passion*

Display of instruments in Bach's house in Leipzig

Title page of the *Clavier-Ubung I*

Clavier Ubung
bestehend in
Præludien, Allemanden, Couranten, Sarabanden, Giquen,
Menuetten, und andern Galanterien;
Denen Liebhabern zur Gemüths Ergoëzung verfertiget
von
Johann Sebastian Bach,
Hochfürstl. Anhalt-Cöthnischen würcklichen Capellmeister und
Directore Chóri Musici Lipsiensis
Partita V.
In Verlegung des Autoris
1730

The instrumental music consists of the following performers:

2 or even 3	violin I
2 or 3	violin 2
2 each	viola 1, 2, cello
1	double-bass
2 or 3, as necessary	oboes
1 or 2	bassoons
3	trumpets
1	drum

In all at least eighteen people for the instruments.

NB Since church music is often composed to include flutes . . . at least two people are needed for them; altogether, then, twenty instrumentalists. The number of performers employed by the City for church music is eight, namely four town pipers, three professional violinists, and one apprentice. Discretion forbids me from speaking truthfully about their competence and musical knowledge; however, I will mention that they are partly retired, and partly not in such good practice as they should be. Here is the list of them: . . . two trumpets, two violins, two oboes and one bassoon. Thus the following players are missing: two players each of first and second violin, viola, cello, and flute; one player of the double-bass. The deficiency here has until now had to be made good partly by the university students but chiefly by the pupils of St Thomas'. The students used to be very willing to do this, in the hope that in time they might . . . receive . . . an honorarium. But as the small payments which came to them have been completely withdrawn, their willingness has similarly disappeared, for who will give his services for nothing? In the absence of more proficient performers, the second violin has been at most times, and the viola, cello and double-bass at all times, played by pupils; it is easy to realise what has been lost to the choir in this way. So far only the Sunday music has been mentioned . . . but if I come to speak of the holy days, when music must be provided for both the principal churches at the same time, the lack of players is even more serious, since I then have to give up . . . pupils who can play an instrument, and do without their help as singers completely.

Further, I cannot forbear mentioning that through the admissions granted until now to so many boys unskilled and ignorant in music, performances have . . . fallen into decline. A boy who knows nothing about music, who cannot even sing a second part . . . can never be any use musically. And even those who bring with them some basic knowledge do not become useful as quickly as I would wish . . . However, no time is allowed to train them . . . as soon as they are admitted, they are put into a choir . . . It is well known that my predecessors, Schelle and Kuhnau, had to fall back on the help of the university students when they wanted to perform complete, good-sounding music, which they were so far warranted in doing that several vocalists, a bass, tenor, alto and instrumentalists . . . were favoured with salaries from the . . . Council, and thus persuaded to strengthen the church music. Now, however, when the present state of music has greatly changed – the art being much advanced and tastes definitely changed, so that old-fashioned music no longer sounds good to our ears – when performers should be chosen to satisfy the present tastes

89

and undertake new kinds of music, and simultaneously to satisfy the composer by their performances of his work, now the few perks have been completely withdrawn from the choir, although they ought to be increased rather than diminished. It is, in any case, astonishing that German musicians should be expected to perform *ex tempore* any kind of music, whether Italian, French, English or Polish, like some of the virtuosos who have studied it for a long time beforehand, even almost knowing it by heart, and who besides have such high salaries that their care and dilligence are well rewarded. This is not taken into account, and our German musicians are left to look after themselves, so that under the need to work for their upkeep, many can never hope to achieve proficiency, much less distinguish themselves . . . The conclusion is easy to see: . . . I am deprived of the ability of getting the music into better shape. Finally I will list the present Foundation Pupils, stating in each case the extent of his musical ability, and leave it for further consideration whether music for instruments and voices can be performed properly under such conditions, or whether a further decline is to be feared . . .
Joh. Seb. Bach.

An incidental value of this letter is the light it casts on contemporary musical practice. But its bluntness betrays Sebastian's intemperance; his shortness with the Council could only increase the mutual animosity.

Sebastian was far from blameless in these controversies. He had often left Leipzig to examine organs elsewhere, or to give inaugural performances; he rarely applied for permission, as he was bound to do. In his seven years as Cantor until this date, he very seldom showed the deference due to his superiors. His activities at the school were particularly open to criticism; although he was employed as both teacher and music director, he concentrated almost all his energies on the latter role. And though his too free behaviour was not totally unprecedented, his truculent impenitence certainly was.

There seems to have been no direct response to his forthright letter. However, fortunately matters considerably improved when, following the death of the incompetent old Rector of the school, Ernesti, a new candidate was appointed in June 1730. The new Rector was Johann Matthias Gesner, sometime Co-rector of the Weimar Gymnasium, and an admirer of Sebastian Bach. He immediately set about improving things at the school of St Thomas'; he tried to tighten up on discipline among the students, and put in hand renovations to the fabric of the school. For the period of his rectorship, at least, there was an armed truce between the Thomas Cantor and the Leipzig City Council.

But so exasperated had Sebastian become with conditions at Leipzig that for a time he considered moving on once again. When he had travelled to Lüneberg in 1700, thirty years earlier, he had been accompanied by a schoolfriend, Georg Erdmann. Sebastian knew that this same man was now Russian agent at Danzig, and wrote to him, pouring out his present troubles, and investigating the possibility of an opening there. That he should suddenly write to a friend from the past about so extreme a move reveals the extent to which Bach had been disturbed by the disagreeable atmosphere in Leipzig. He listed his grievances at Leipzig:

Johann Mathias Gesner
(1691-1761)

IOHANNES MATTHIAS GESNERVS
natus CIƆIƆCLXXXXI. *moritur*
TOΠΑΡΟΝΕΥΠΟΙΕΙΝ

Since I find (1) that this appointment is by no means as advantageous as it
was described to me,
(2) that many fees incidental to it are now stopped,
(3) that the town is a very expensive place to live in,
(4) that the authorities are very odd people, with little love of music, so that
I live amidst almost continual vexation, jealousy and persecution, I feel
compelled to seek, with God's help, my fortune elsewhere . . . My present
position amounts to about 700 thaler, and when there are more funerals
than usual, the fees rise proportionately; but when a healthy wind blows,
they fall as for example last year, when I lost fees that would normally
come in from funerals to the amount of over 100 thaler. In Thuringia, I
could survive better on 400 thaler than I can here on twice that amount,
since the cost of living is so high.

He adds, more happily, a note on his family:

They are all born musicians, and I can assure you that I can already form
both a choir and an instrumental ensemble from my family, particularly
since my present wife sings a good, clear soprano, and my eldest daughter,
too, joins in quite competently.

But this mood of despair with the situation in Leipzig passed before
Sebastian could take steps to make a move.

9 The Years of Maturity: Leipzig 1730-4

Johann Matthias Gesner brought a new spirit of learning and conciliation to the school of St Thomas. As a scholar he pioneered Classical philology; as a teacher, he brought enthusiasm and learning to the post of Rector. He implemented plans for renewing the school buildings, which entailed the whole teaching staff finding temporary alternative accommodation. The Bach family probably moved to the home of Dr Christoph Dendorf, near to his brewery in Leipzig.

Two more storeys were added to the school buildings, bringing an immediate improvement in facilities. But Gesner also overhauled the running of the school. Music was given a vital place in the curriculum; in his characteristically Classical style of argument, Gesner explained to the boys that praising God in music linked them with the heavenly choirs; they should be eager to give up leisure-time to practise for musical performances. He imposed fines to persuade the unconvinced.

Gesner made life much more tolerable for Sebastian, who was released from any teaching duties apart from music, and was put in charge of the daily trips to the morning service at St Thomas' and St Nicholas', where a group of eight boys sang on alternate days. Gesner also ensured that Bach obtained all the fees and monies due to him for his various activities. At last Sebastian could work in an atmosphere of relative peace.

But Gesner later moved on to Göttingen, where he worked, among other things, on a Latin commentary of the Roman author Quintilian. He included a light-hearted comparison of Bach with the Classical lyre-player:

All these (outstanding achievements) . . . you would reckon trivial could you rise from the dead and see our Bach . . . how, with both hands and using all his fingers, he plays a clavier which apparently consists of many citharas in one, or runs over the keys of the king of instruments, whose

Page from the manuscript of the *Coffee Cantata*

Johann Sebastian Bach

Canon dedicated to Gesner

innumerable pipes are made to sound by means of bellows; and how, going in one direction with his hands, and in another direction, at the utmost speed, with his feet, he conjures up unaided . . . hosts of harmonious sounds; I say, could you but see him, how he achieves what a number of your cithara players and 600 performers on reed instruments could never achieve, not merely . . . singing and playing at the same time his own parts, but presiding over thirty or forty musicians at once, controlling this one with a nod, another with a stamp of his foot, a third with a warning finger, keeping time and tune, giving a high note to one, a low to another, and notes in between to the rest. This one man, standing by himself in the middle of the loud sounds, having the hardest task of all, can tell at any moment if anyone goes astray, and can keep all the musicians in order, restore any waverer to certainty and stop him from going wrong. Rhythm is in his every limb, he takes in all the harmonies by his subtle ear and voices all the different parts through his own mouth. . . . I . . . reckon this Bach of mine to comprise in himself many Orpheuses and twenty Arions.

It is interesting that Gesner dwells on Bach's skills as a conductor and performer rather than as a composer. In this same period Sebastian seems to have discovered a small corps of particularly fine singers, such as Johann Ludwig Krebs, son of one of Sebastian's

View of Neustadt,
Dresden (Canaletto)

Weimar pupils, Christoph Nickelmann and Christian Friedrich Schemelli.

About twenty years before Bach's arrival in Leipzig, the brilliant young Georg Telemann had been a student at the university. In 1704 he was appointed organist of the New Church, and attracted many of his fellow-students there as singers and instrumentalists. The upshot was his formation of the *Collegium Musicum* – a kind of musical society, which met for weekly rehearsals, practising in the open-air in summer, and in a coffee-house in winter. They played publicly during the year, performing secular cantatas and orchestral music. Telemann even began operatic work with this enthusiastic group of musicians, much to the disapproval of Kuhnau, the Thomas Cantor. Although Telemann left soon afterwards, the activities of the *Collegium Musicum* continued, although opera faded out.

In 1729, GB Schott, who had presided over the *Collegium Musicum*, left Leipzig, leaving Bach free to take over the direction of this association, and of a second similar group which had sprung up. The two groups performed regularly at Leipzig coffee-houses, particularly at Zimmermann's, giving them good practice, and keeping them in the public eye, to the enhancement of their career prospects. Their immediate financial reward was apparently minimal, although Sebastian certainly secured a regular fee for his services from the proprietor. It was probably such performance opportunities which stimulated Bach to compose some of his secular cantatas: for example *The Contest between Phoebus and Pan*, with its text by Picander, the librettist for the *St Matthew Passion*, based on a passage in Ovid's *Metamorphoses*. Sebastian used this vehicle to pour ridicule upon new musical fashions. In a singing contest, Pan stands for new styles, Midas prefers his ridiculous song, and is given ass's ears for his pains. Pan's song is simple and rather crude; the winning song, that scored for Phoebus, is intricate rhythmically, and scored sensitively for strings, flute and oboe d'amore.

A second well-known example of Bach's more bucolic style is another light-hearted work, *The Coffee Cantata*, first performed in 1732 by the *Collegium Musicum*. An old 'stick-in-the-mud' is concerned about his daughter's new addiction to coffee. He tries to wean her from the habit by threats and promises, and thinks he has succeeded when he promises to bribe her with a husband. But the wily daughter has the last word; she stipulates that her husband must allow her to drink coffee to her heart's content. Bach matches music to words by treating the cantata as an oratorio, with arias, recitatives, and having the main narrative recounted by an and recitatives, and having the main narrative recounted by an blown characters in the father and his self-willed daughter Liesgen.

Bach's Letter of Dedication to Frederick Augustus of Saxony, to accompany the *Kyrie* and *Gloria*

pṡ. den 19. Aug. 1733.

Durchlauchtigster Churfürst,

Gnädigster Herr,

Ew. Königl. Hoheit überreiche in tieffster Devotion gegenwärtige geringe Arbeit von derjenigen Wißenschafft, welche ich in der Musique erlanget, mit gantz unterthänigster bitte, Sie wollen dieselbe nicht nach der schlechten Composition, sondern nach Dero Welt berühmten Clemenz mit gnädigsten Augen ansehen, und mich darbey in Dero mächtigste Protection zu nehmen geruhen. Ich habe einige Jahre und biß daher bey denen beyden Haupt-Kirchen in Leipzig das Directorium in der Music gehabt, darbey aber ein und andere Bekränckung unverschuldt, iedoch iezuweilen auch eine Verminderung deren mit solcher Function verknüpfften Acci-dentien aussehen müßen, welches aber gäntz-

Undoubtedly this cantata went down splendidly with its coffee-house audience.

Later, for his rustic *Peasant Cantata* (1742), Sebastian adapted a much simpler, vernacular style, employing the styles of such dances as the Polonaise, the Mazurka, the Bourrée, and folk songs as arias. The whole piece, written for the new Lord of the Manor of two villages neighbouring Leipzig, was economically scored for violin, viola and double-bass, soprano and bass.

1 February 1733, Augustus II, the Elector of Saxony, died. His son was crowned King of Poland on 27 January 1734, becoming a Catholic for reasons of state. His accession precipitated a number of compositions from Sebastian, who knew that the new monarch was favourably disposed towards the arts. He wrote four cantatas for the royal family, and finally excelled himself for the occasion of Augustus' visit to Leipzig on 21 April 1733, to accept the oath of allegiance. Bach was commissioned by the loyal City Council to write a *Kyrie* and *Gloria* for performance at St Nicholas', to sandwich the sermon. Taking the period of official mourning to work on the pieces, Sebastian wrote the *Kyrie* as a mourning-piece for the dead Elector, the *Gloria* as a celebration of his successor. Ironically, the Elector, as a Catholic, did not actually hear the first performance of the work in the Lutheran church.

Apparently Sebastian was encouraged to pursue the possibility of advancement with the new Elector by expanding his composition into a mass for the coronation of Augustus III in Dresden. This was completed to become the great *B Minor Mass;* although it was presented to Augustus, it was not performed at this time. Probably this was finally in the best interests of its composer; the querulous Leipzigers might well have objected strongly to their Musical Director's writing a Catholic Mass.

In the *B Minor Mass*, Bach reaches into a mysterious remoteness of spirituality, though often using material originating in previous works of his own. In a way, he seems to have been working towards a universal Christian statement; for instance, he opens and closes the *Credo* with Gregorian chant melodies.

But Sebastian's was not a one-shot campaign. He wrote a cantata for Augustus' name-day, possibly adapted from a piece written to celebrate the re-opening of the school of St Thomas in 1732; he composed a second cantata for the birthday of the heir to the throne; and a third for the Queen-Electress. However, Sebastian did not squander his work on these pieces; much of the material was re-employed in the *Christmas Oratorio* of 1734.

When Bach submitted his *Kyrie* and *Gloria* to Augustus, he sent with them a letter asking for recognition:

Wilhelm Friedemann Bach
(1710-1784)

For some years and until the present time I have held the Directorship of

An early pianoforte

The first page of music
for Part III of the *Clavier
Ubung*

Music in the two main churches of Leipzig, but have innocently suffered various injuries and on occasion the reducing of fees due to me in this office; these grievances would disappear if your Majesty would favour me by bestowing the title of Your Highness' Court Capelle.
(27 July 1733)

But it was not until November 1736, following the submission of yet another cantata, that Augustus issued a certificate recognising Bach as 'Composer to the Royal Court Capelle'.

Sebastian now had other connections with Dresden too. He played the organ at St Sophia's there early in the 1730s, and when, in June 1733, the post of organist fell vacant, he suggested for the post his son Wilhelm Friedemann, who was now twenty-three. He performed so well at the trial that he secured the job, giving Sebastian all the more reason to visit Dresden occasionally.

In Bach's time, the word 'clavier' was used to cover any keyboard instrument, including even the organ. Mostly, it refers to one of the three main types of stringed keyboard instrument: the harpsichord, with its one or two manuals, and strings plucked by quill or leather; the spinet, with one manual and one set of strings, plucked by quill

Title Page of the Third Part of the *Clavier-Übung*

101

or leather; and the clavichord, with a single manual, one set of strings, struck by thin pieces of metal. The pianoforte, though in existence, was probably only used in Sebastian's late *Musical Offering*. Normally Bach showed no preference for any particular keyboard instrument. In the *Goldberg Variations* and the *Italian Concerto*, however, he did specifically ask for a harpsichord.

One of the activities Sebastian took more seriously during his Leipzig period was the publishing of his works. In 1726, soon after settling in Leipzig, he published his first 'Clavier Suite', later called a Partita, 'consisting of Preludes, Allemandes, Courantes, Sarabandes, Gigues, Minuets and other Galanteries'. One copy was dedicated to Prince Leopold's first child by his second wife.

> *Serene and Gracious Prince, though cradle cov'rings deck thee*
> *Yet doth thy Princely glance show thee more than full-grown.*
> *Forgive me, pray, if I from slumber should awake thee.*
> *The while my playful page to thee doth homage own.*

The published editions of Bach's music were sold in Leipzig by Sebastian himself, and by his two eldest sons in the towns where they were respectively working. In 1731 the complete set of six Partitas was published. In 1735 Bach published Part II of his Clavier works, again selling direct to the public, but also acting through the publisher Christoph Weigel of Nuremberg. A third part was published in 1739, containing organ music. By now Bach was regularly publishing: the *Goldberg Variations* were regarded as Part IV of the same keyboard series when they were printed in 1742. Finally Sebastian published his *Musical Offering* in 1747.

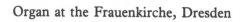
Organ at the Frauenkirche, Dresden

731 | 385 VII
132
382 | 258
118 II 76

Organ at the Sophienkirche, Dresden

Johann Sebastian Bach

Page from the first printed score of the *Musical Offering*

10 New Trials:
Leipzig 1734-40

In 1734, after only four years as Rector, Johann Matthias Gesner left Leipzig to take a chair at the new University of Göttingen. He was succeeded at the school by Johann August Ernesti, vice-principal since 1731. The new young Rector, only twenty-seven when he took up the post, was an accomplished scholar, determined to raise academic standards at the school, and to redirect the balance of studies towards more modern subjects and away from classics and theology. Ernesti made no secret of the fact that he ranked music with these outmoded subjects – particularly the increasingly unfashionable style of the Thomas Cantor, Sebastian Bach.

Although there were the seeds of future problems here, Sebastian was well-disposed enough to make the young Ernesti godfather to Johann Christian, the 'London' Bach, in 1735. Other members of the family were now beginning to leave home. Carl Philipp Emanuel went off to study law at Frankfurt am Oder in 1734; in 1735 Johann Gottfried Bernhard took up the post of organist at St Mary's Church, Mühlhausen, backed by the recommendation of his father:

My youngest son, Johann Gottfried Bach, has already acquired such skill in music that I am firmly convinced that he is fully equipped and able to attend to this newly vacant post of town organist . . .

But the careers of Ernesti and Bach were set on collision course; the crash came in 1736, and the dispute dragged on tediously for two years. It is perhaps best summarised by a contemporary historian:

With Ernesti, Bach fell out completely. The occasion was as follows. Ernesti removed the General Prefect Krause for having beaten one of the younger students too vigorously, expelled him from the school when he fled, and chose another student in his place as General Prefect – a right that really belongs to the Cantor, whom the General Prefect has to represent. Because the student chosen was no use in performing church music, Bach

104

made a different choice. The situation between him and Ernesti developed into charge and countercharge, and from that time on the two men were enemies. Bach began to hate the students who devoted themselves completely to the humanities and treated music as a secondary matter; and Ernesti became a foe of music. When he came upon a student practising an instrument, he would exclaim 'What, you want to be a beer-fiddler too?' By virtue of the high regard in which he was held by the Burgomaster, Stieglitz, he managed to get released from the duties of the special inspection of the school, and to have them assigned to a fourth colleague. Thus when it was Bach's turn to undertake the inspection, he quoted the precedent of Ernesti, and came neither to table nor to prayers; and this neglect of duty had the worst influence on the moral training of the students.

Sebastian had recourse to the Council, complaining in August 1736:

The present Rector, Magister Johann August Ernesti, has, as a new departure, tried to have the prefect of the first choir replaced without my previous knowledge and consent . . . He has refused to withdraw this appointment despite all the protests that I, in complete good will, have made to him.

In less than a week, Sebastian addressed four long, closely-argued letters to the City Council, complaining about Ernesti's behaviour. Ernesti for his part answered back in kind, averring that Sebastian was untrustworthy and venal. Sebastian went on to appeal to the Leipzig Consistory and, meeting no satisfaction, finally appealed to the King. By now Bach was recognised as Royal Polish and Electoral Saxon Court Composer, and met some response from his patron.

Certainly there is no further reference to this acrimonious dispute in the official records. But this is not an entirely good sign. We do know that Ernesti continued to undermine music in the school, while Bach became less and less dutiful in the execution of his tasks. In 1740 the school authorities had to appoint a new master to teach musical theory; Bach was simply not fulfilling his duties. Even his musical output apparently diminished; he was composing noticeably fewer new works, the choirs were now performing more previously-written material.

But this should not be taken to mean that Bach became generally idle. The performances with the *Collegium Musicum* continued. We have a record of the announcement of the 1736 series of concerts:

Both the public musical concerts or Assemblies that are held here weekly are still flourishing steadily. One is conducted by Mr Sebastian Bach, Capellmeister to the Court of Weissenfels and Musical Director at St

105

Thomas' and St Nicholas' Churches in this city, and is held, except during the Fair, once a week in Zimmermann's coffee-house in the Luther Strasse, on Friday evenings from 8 to 10 o'clock; during the fair, however, twice a week, on Tuesdays and Fridays, at the same time . . . The participants in these musical concerts are chiefly students here, among whom there are always good musicians, so that sometimes they become, as is known famous virtuosos.

This is indicative of a trend for Bach. He seems to have become rather less interested in church music. This is perhaps a reflection of the growing strength of Enlightenment thinking in Germany. It has frequently been suggested that Sebastian's religious fervour cooled towards the end of his life. Certainly his attention seems to have become increasingly taken up with instrumental works, and with getting his compositions published.

Sebastian also kept up his busy programme of travelling to test organs and to meet fellow-musicians. He paid a number of visits to Dresden. We have a newspaper report of one such occasion:

On 1 December 1736, the famous Capellmeister to the Prince of Saxe-Weissenfels, and Director of Music at Leipzig, Mr Johann Sebastian Bach, performed from two to four o'clock on the new organ in the church of Our Lady in the presence of the Russian Ambassador . . . and many persons of rank.

This was the occasion on which the King named Sebastian 'His Majesty's Composer'.

But troubles rarely came singly to Sebastian. In 1737, too, he was attacked by a fellow musician, Johann Adolf Scheibe, the musical son of a famous organ-builder, who had been commended by Sebastian six years earlier as 'a most zealous student of music'. He had launched a magazine entitled *The Critical Musician*, in which he attacked Sebastian's compositions:

A musical composition must naturally be pleasant and tickle the ear, it must also please the reason . . . Musicians must think naturally, reasonably and sublimely . . . This great man would be the wonder of the universe if his compositions displayed more agreeable qualities, were less turgid and sophisticated, more simple and natural in character. His music is extremely difficult to play because the efficiency of his own limbs sets his standard; he expects singers and players to be as agile with voice and instrument as he is with his fingers, which is impossible. Grace-notes and embellishments, such as a player instinctively supplies, he puts down in actual symbols, a habit which not only sacrifices the harmonic beauty of his music, but also blurs its melodic line. All his parts, too, are equally melodic, so that one cannot distinguish the principal tune among them.

This is clearly an attack by a Young Turk on the old-fashioned

The Market-place, Halle

work of a master – but no more acceptable for that. Bach did in fact have his defenders. A friend at the university, Johann Abraham Birnbaum, penned a lengthy pamphlet supporting him; one of the

Collegium Musicum members, Christoph Lorenz Mizler, pointed
out that Sebastian was perfectly capable of composing in a modern
style.

Though this attack must have hurt Sebastian, it seems not to have
been merely malicious. Later, in 1739, Scheibe wrote a handsome
commendation of Sebastian's *Italian Concerto:*

It would take as great a master of music as Mr Bach, who has almost alone
taken possession of the clavier, and with whom we can certainly defy
foreign nations, to provide us with such a piece in this form of
composition – a piece which deserves emulation by all our great
composers, and which will be imitated totally in vain by foreigners.

At the end of the 1730s we begin to get more light on the Bach
household. Johann Elias Bach, thirty-three-year-old relative of
Sebastian, came as a lodger in 1737. The younger man's letters give
us fascinating glimpses of the Bachs in Leipzig. He helped the
Cantor by drafting letters for him, though he was in Leipzig
primarily to study theology. He also helped as tutor to Anna
Magdalena's three sons.

In 1739 we find Elias writing on Sebastian's behalf to the Cantor
of Ronneberg, asking him to subscribe to the publication of the
third part of the Clavier Works. On a more personal note, we find
Elias writing to Cantor Hiller at Glanchau near Halle, asking about
the possibility of buying a singing bird:

Bach . . . when he came back from Halle . . . reported to his beloved wife

109

110

. . . that Your Honour possessed a linnet, which, as a result of skilful instruction by its master, made itself heard in most pleasant singing. Now since the honoured lady, my cousin, particularly loves such birds, I wanted to ask whether Your Honour would be willing to release this singing bird to her for a reasonable sum.

The fact that Elias is responsible for letters of this kind suggests the possibility that Anna Magdalena was only marginally literate. In another letter on her behalf, Elias writes to a Mr von Mayer in Halle to acknowledge a present of six carnations:

With an extended description of the joy which was given by them . . . I will not burden Your Honour, but will mention only this: that she values this deserved gift more highly than children do their Christmas presents, and tends them with such care as is usually given to children, lest a single one wither.

But the irritable relationship with the Leipzig authorities continued. We find that Bach was warned about his Passion music for Good Friday 1739. The Council Clerk recorded:

I have gone to Mr Bach here and pointed out . . . that the music he intends to perform next Good Friday should be omitted until normal permission is given. He replied that it had always been done in this way; he didn't care, for he got nothing out of it anyway, and it was only a burden; . . . if an objection were made on account of the test, it had already been performed several times.

The difficulties appear to have been caused by two intransigent parties: the Council made little attempt to honour its celebrated Cantor; Sebastian did little or nothing to soften his attitudes.

Meanwhile we find Johann Elias requesting his sister to send ten or twelve measures of new sweet wine as a gift for Sebastian's family for staying at their house for two years; while Sebastian writes thanking Johann Schneider, financial officer to the Duke of Weissenfels, for a generous gift of venison in July 1741.

But Anna Magdalena was not in good health. In 1741 Sebastian visited Carl Philipp Emanuel in Berlin; Johann Elias had to write to tell him of Anna Magdalena's illness:

Our most lovable Mama has been sick for a week now, and we do not know whether perhaps as a result of the violent throbbing of her pulse a creeping fever or other serious condition may arise.

Only four days later, Elias wrote again:

Great must be the pain we feel about the increasing weakness of our most honoured Mama, for she has now gone a fortnight without a single night with more than an hour's sleep, and can neither sit up nor lie down, so that last night I was called, and we feared, to our great sorrow, we would lose her.

Matters were not quite as serious as he feared; but certainly Anna Magdalena's health was a continuing problem. She refused an invitation to Weissenfels on the grounds that her family feared that her continuing weakness might finally end fatally if she undertook such a journey.

In 1742, Johann Elias left the Cantor's household to become Cantor at Schweinfurth. He wrote to thank his cousin for his happy time in Leipzig; with his departure, his affectionate letters, giving more intimate glimpses of the Bach household, cease.

Manuscript of the beginning of the E-major Fugue from "The Well-Tempered Clavier"

Bust of J.S. Bach

Page from the manuscript of the chorale prelude "Der tag, der ist so freudenreich"

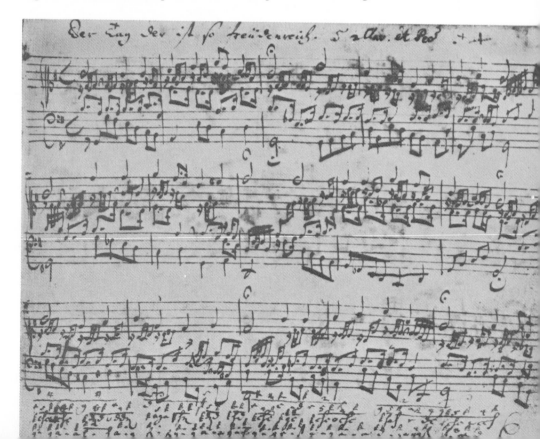

11 The Last Years: Leipzig 1740-50

Bach continued to write original compositions in his last years; but, as we have seen, he devoted much energy to revising and completing earlier work. It was in these years that he built on the *Kyrie* and *Gloria* of 1733 to produce the magnificent *B Minor Mass.*

Following the publication of the third part of his Clavier works, there appeared the fourth part in 1742. This was, in fact, a single work, an 'aria with thirty variations', written for Sebastian's pupil, Goldberg. It was the most complex and compact of Bach's clavier works, with an amazing, soaring style. Because of its origin, the piece is often popularly referred to as the 'Goldberg Variations', and combines with supreme virtuosity the tightest of logical order and the freest expressiveness. The 'Goldberg Variations' were actually commissioned by Baron von Kaiserling, the Russian Ambassador to the court in Dresden; Goldberg was his harpsichordist as well as Bach's pupil.

It was in 1742 too that Sebastian published the second volume of his 'Well-Tempered Clavier'. Just as the first volume of preludes and fugues was first put together as a teaching aid for Maria Barbara's family, the second volume probably originated as music for Anna Magdalena's family.

Bach's examinations of new organs continued. In 1746 he reported on the organ at Zschortau, which had been built by Johann Scheibe of Leipzig. Sebastian was in this case particularly complimentary about the organ builder's workmanship. In the case of the organ of St Wenceslaus, Naumburg, Sebastian stipulated:

It will be necessary that the organ-builder be requested to go over the entire organ once again, from stop to stop, watching out for greater equality of voicing, and of key and stop action . . .

In his collection of six chorales, published by a pupil, Georg Schüller, in 1746 or later, Sebastian shows a new face. For the first time he looks forward, and introduces elements from the younger generation of composers. Perhaps this was mainly to achieve a popular acceptance; certainly there is a new tone to be heard.

But in 1740 Carl Philipp Emanuel was made accompanist at the court of Frederick the Great of Prussia in Berlin; he even had the privilege of accompanying at the harpsichord the first flute solo that Frederick played as King. Frederick was renowned for his artistic patronage, and Bach is probably the originator of the remark that 'at Berlin, the golden age of music seemed to be inaugurated'. He first visited Emanuel in Berlin in 1741, but further visits were made difficult by political conditions until later in the decade. By then, Hermann von Kaiserling, recipient of Bach's 'Goldberg Variations', was Russian Ambassador at Berlin, and procured an invitation for Bach from the King. Sebastian travelled to Berlin in the spring of 1747, and had the added joy of seeing his first grandson, Johann August, who had been born 30 November 1745. Sebastian tried out all the forte pianos at Frederick's palace, and greatly impressed the King, as a contemporary newspaper report indicates:

A Silbermann Grand Piano, from the original used by J S Bach at Potsdam

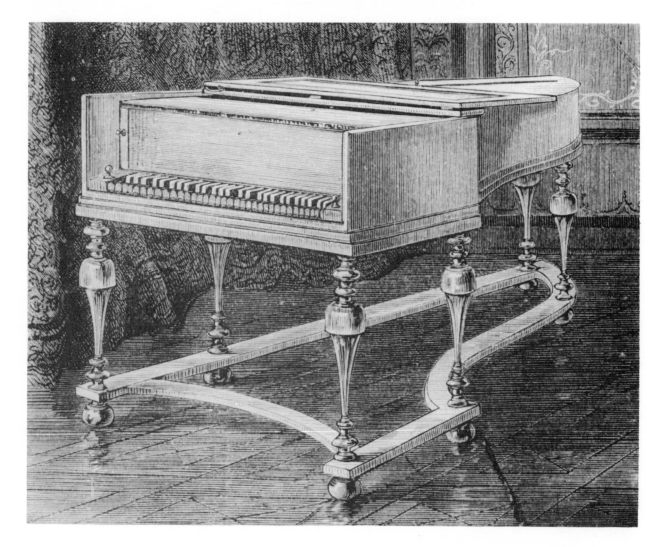

We hear from Potsdam that last Sunday the famous Capellmeister from Leipzig, Mr Bach, arrived with the intention of hearing the excellent Royal music at the palace. In the evening, at about the time when the regular chamber music in the Royal apartments usually begins, His Majesty was informed that Capellmeister Bach had arrived . . . His August self immediately gave orders for Bach to be admitted, and, when he entered, went to the fortepiano, condescending to play without preparation a theme to be treated as a fugue by Capellmeister Bach. This was done so well that not only was His Majesty pleased to show his satisfaction, but everybody present was astonished. Mr Bach found the theme so beautiful that he intends to write a regular fugue for engraving.

Sebastian was as good as his word. The outcome of Frederick's subject was Bach's magnificent 'Musical Offering' – consisting of a three-part fugue, a six-part fugue, two sets of five canons, and a sonata in four movements. Sebastian recalled the occasion of its conception:

I still remember the very special Royal Grace when, some time ago, during my visit to Potsdam, Your Majesty deigned to play me a theme for a fugue on the clavier, and graciously requested me to carry it out . . . I soon noticed, however, that in the absence of necessary preparation, the execution of the task did not go as well as such a fine theme demanded. I resolved therefore and promptly pledged myself to work out this right Royal theme more fully, and then make it known to the world.

Sebastian seems to have been very pleased with his labours; he printed one hundred copies in the first instance, most of which he distributed as gifts to various friends. There is no record, however, that Frederick gave him any financial reward for these efforts.

Touchingly, the last surviving letter of Sebastian concerned domestic matters. He writes to Johann Elias at Schweinfurth:

For the delectable cask of wine that came . . . accept my best thanks. Unfortunately the cask suffered a jolt, or some other accident, on the journey, for on examination it was found to be one-third empty and contains, the Inspector declares, only six quarts. It is regrettable that the smallest drop of such a noble gift of God should be wasted . . . It is unfortunate that we live so far apart, otherwise I should have the pleasure of inviting you to my daughter Lizzie's wedding, which takes place in January 1749, to the new organist at Naumburg, Herr Altnickel.

Altnickel was also a violinist, singer and composer, a former pupil of Sebastian's. The newly-weds christened their first child Johann Sebastian in honour of his grandfather.

Sebastian's final major composition was *The Art of the Fugue,* which was in fact not completed, although part of it had already been engraved before his death. What remains of it is a staggering

Frederick the Great
playing the flute at a
chamber concert at Sans
Souci, Potsdam

Frederick the Great
(1712-86)

A page from the original
edition of the *Art of the
Fugue*, 1751

achievement, and appears to follows logically from the *Musical Offering*. Sebastian gives no indication of what instrument it was written for. It is written in open score probably with no specific instruments in mind as an example of 'pure' fugue technique.

But Sebastian's health was beginning to fail rapidly. It is possible that by mid-1749 he had already suffered a stroke. As early as this, the Leipzig City Council was discussing a possible successor to him, in the event of his death. Count von Brühl, a minister at the court at Dresden, recommended a man named Gottlob Harrer as the new Thomas Cantor, and on 8 June 1749:

The Musical Offering in Bach's manuscript

by order of A Noble and Most Wise Council of this Town, most of whom were present, the trial performance for the future appointment as Cantor of St Thomas', in case the Capellmeister and Cantor, Mr Sebastian Bach, should die, was given at the Three Swans on the river Brühl by Mr Gottlob Harrer, Capell Director . . . with the greatest applause.

Sans Souci, Potsdam

Although this was insensitively premature, Bach's eyesight was giving him increasing problems. Weak-sighted for years, through heredity, overwork and poor lighting, by 1749 Sebastian was almost blind. In 1750 the English oculist, Chevalier John Taylor, happened to be in Leipzig, and performed two unsuccessful operations on the composer's eyes. Although Sebastian apparently struggled on, still trying to write new material, he died 28 July, just ten days after his sight was unexpectedly and suddenly restored. His death was the immediate result of a second stroke, which was rapidly followed by a fierce fever.

The Council remained unsympathetic to the end. Laconic comments such as 'Bach was certainly a good musician, but no school teacher', and 'The school needs a Cantor, not a Conductor' followed his death. they soon appointed Harrer; a 'very quiet and accommodating' man.

It is remarkable that Sebastian left no will. He was notable for his methodical nature; but his estate was divided between his nine surviving children and his widow, Anna Magdalena. The Council was characteristically tight-fisted in calculating the relief due to Bach's widow; and only Carl Philipp Emanuel appears to have been of much practical assistance to her – by helping educate the young Johann Christian. Anna Magdalena now became an almshouse resident, until her death in February 1760.

120

A later portrait of Bach

Manuscript page from *The Art of the Fugue*

Petition from Anna Magdalena Bach

Her signature: "Anna Magdalena Bach, widow"

Sebastian's death was announced from the pulpit of St Thomas':

Peacefully and blissfully departed in God the Esteemed and Highly Respected Mr Johann Sebastian Bach, Court Composer to his Royal Majesty in Poland and Serene Electoral Highness in Saxony, as well as Capellmeister to the Prince of Anhalt-Cöthen, and Cantor in St Thomas' School, at the Square of St Thomas'.

An obituary of Sebastian was written by Carl Philipp Emanuel and Johann Friedrich Agricola, and published in 1754. After an account of the composer's life, it gave an assessment of his musical achievement:

If ever a composer showed polyphony in its greatest strength, it was certainly our late lamented Bach. If ever a musician used the most concealed mysteries of harmony with the greatest artistry, it was certainly our Bach. No one ever showed so many ingenious and unusual ideas as he in elaborate pieces, which normally seem dry exercises in craftsmanship. He needed only to hear a theme to be aware – it seemed instantaneously – of almost every intricacy an artist could produce in treating it. His melodies were unusual, but always varied, rich in invention, and like those of no other composer. His serious temperament attracted him to music that was serious, elaborate and profound; but he could also, when appropriate, adjust himself, especially as a performer, to a lighter and more humorous approach. His constant practice at working out polyphonic pieces gave his eye such facility that even with the largest scores he could take in all the simultaneous parts at a glance. His hearing was so fine that he could detect the slightest error even in the largest ensembles. It is only a pity that it was seldom that he was lucky enough to find a group of performers who could spare him unpleasant discoveries of this kind.

As a conductor, he was very accurate, and he was unusually assured of the tempo, which he generally took very lively.

As long as we are only contradicted with the mere supposition of possibly better organists and clavier players, we cannot be blamed for declaring boldly that Bach was the greatest organist and clavier player we have ever had. Maybe many famous men have achieved much in polyphony; but are they as skilful in both hands and feet as Bach was? This doubt will not be considered baseless by anybody who had the pleasure of hearing him, and who is not carried away with prejudice . . .

How extraordinary, how novel, how expressive, how beautiful were his ideas as an improviser. How perfectly he realised them. All his fingers were equally skilled; equally capable of the utmost accuracy in performance. He had worked out such a convenient system of fingering that he easily overcame the greatest difficulties with utter fluency. Before Bach, the most celebrated clavier players of Germany and other countries rarely used the thumb. He certainly knew how to use it. With both feet, he could play things with the pedals which many skilled clavier players would find hard enough playing with five fingers. He not only understood the art of playing the organ, combining its various stops most skilfully, and

displaying the peculiar character of each stop with perfection; but he also knew about the construction of the organ, from one end to the other. This he demonstrated particularly on one occasion, at the trial of a new organ in a church near where his mortal remains now lie. The builder of this organ was in the final years of a long life. The trial was possibly one of the most exacting ever made. Thus the complete approval which Bach accorded to the instrument did great honour both to the organ-builder and . . . to Bach himself.

Twenty years later, Philip Emanuel reminisced more widely about his father:

The exact tuning of his own instruments, and of the whole orchestra, had his greatest attention. No one could tune and quill his instruments to his satisfaction; he did it all himself. The positioning of an orchestra he understood perfectly. He made good use of any space. He grasped at first glance any peculiarity of a room. A remarkable illustration of this follows:

He came to Berlin to visit me; I showed him the new opera house. He saw at once its virtues and defects, with regard to the sound of music in it. I showed him the great dining hall; we climbed up to the gallery that runs round the upper part of the hall. He looked at the ceiling, and without further investigation stated that the architect had unintentionally accomplished a remarkable feat, without anyone realising. If somebody went to one corner of the rectangular hall and whispered very softly upwards against the wall, somebody standing in the diagonally opposite corner, with his face to the wall, would hear what was said quite clearly, while between them, and elsewhere in the room, nobody would hear a thing . . . This was caused by the arches in the vaulted ceiling, which he noticed immediately.

He heard the slightest wrong note even in very large ensembles. As the greatest expert and judge of harmony, he preferred playing the viola, with appropriate dynamics. In his youth, and until he was approaching old age, he played the violin cleanly and penetratingly, and with it controlled the orchestra better than he could have done from the harpsichord. He perfectly understood the potential of all the stringed instruments, as evidenced by his solos for violin and cello without accompanying bass. One of the greatest violinists told me once he had come across no better music for training good violinists . . .

Thanks to his skill at harmonising, on more than one occasion he accompanied trios on the spur of the moment and, being in a good mood, and knowing the composer would not object, using the sparse continuo part placed in front of him, converted them into complete quartets, amazing their composer.

When he listened to a rich and multi-voiced fugue, after the first entries of the subjects he could tell what counterpoint devices could be applied, and which the composer ought to apply. On such occasions, when I was standing next to him, and he had told me his surmises, he would joyfully nudge me when his forecasts were fulfilled.

He had a good penetrating voice, with a wide range, and a pleasant manner of singing.

123

Goethe's house, Weimar

Almost before he died, Sebastian was outmoded. None of his works was deemed fit for publication for fifty years after his death. He was considered unfashionable by the new generation of composers.

It took musicians to rediscover a master-musician. Mozart apparently heard Bach's motet *Singet dem Herrn ein neues Lied* with a shock: 'What is this? Now there is something we can learn from.' It was ironically Beethoven's brilliant playing of the 'Well-Tempered Clavier' that first gained him a reputation as a virtuoso performer in Vienna.

Gradually Bach's works began to appear in print. In nineteenth century England, such men as Samuel Sebastian Wesley tried to bring Bach to a new public. Goethe was another great admirer of JS Bach. But it was under Mendelssohn in 1829 that the *St Matthew Passion* was performed again.

Felix Mendelssohn

125

A Bach Chronology

1685 Born at Eisenach to Johann Ambrosius Bach

1694 Bach's mother, Elisabeth, dies

1695 Bach's father, Johann Ambrosius, dies. Bach goes to Ohrdruf to live with his brother Johann Christoph

1700 Goes to join the choir of St Michael's, Lüneberg

1702 Goes to Hamburg to hear the organist Reinken

1703 Violinist to Duke Johann Ernst of Weimar
Goes to take the post of organist at the New Church, Arnstadt

1706 Trouble with Arnstadt consistory

1707 Appointed organist at St Blaise, Mühlhausen.
Marries Maria Barbara

1708 Writes cantata *Gott ist mein König*
Appointed court organist to Duke Wilhelm Ernst of Saxe Weimar.
Birth of Catharina Dorothea

1710 Wilhelm Friedemann born

1714 Carl Philipp Emanuel born

1715 Johann Gottfried Bernhard born

1718 Takes post of concert master to Prince Leopold of Anhalt-Cöthen

1720 Maria Barbara dies

1721 Brandenburg Concertos
Marries Anna Magdalena

1722 *Clavierbüchlein* for Anna Magdalena
Part I of the *Well-Tempered Clavier*

1723 Becomes Thomas Cantor, Leipzig
First performance of *St John Passion*

1725 *Note Book* for Anna Magdalena

1729 First performance of *St Matthew Passion*

1732 Johann Christoph Friedrich born

1733 Visits Dresden

1734 First performance of *Christmas Oratorio*
1736 Dispute with Ernesti
1744 Part II of the *Well-Tempered Clavier*
1747 Visits Frederick the Great at Potsdam
The Musical Offering
1748 *The Art of the Fugue*
1750 Dies, 28 July
1829 Mendelssohn revives *St Matthew Passion*

Further Reading

Alec Robertson: *Bach: A Concertgoer's Companion*, Clive Bingley, London, 1977

Ed Hans T. David and Arthur Mendel, *The Bach Reader*, JM Dent, London, 1966

Imogen Holst, *Bach*, Faber, London 1965

Werner Neumann: *Bach, A pictorial biography*, Thames and Hudson, London, 1961

CS Terry: *Bach: A biography*, OUP, 1932

CS Terry: *The Music of Bach*, OUP 1933, paperback Dover, 1963

Bach's sarcophagus in the Johanniskirche

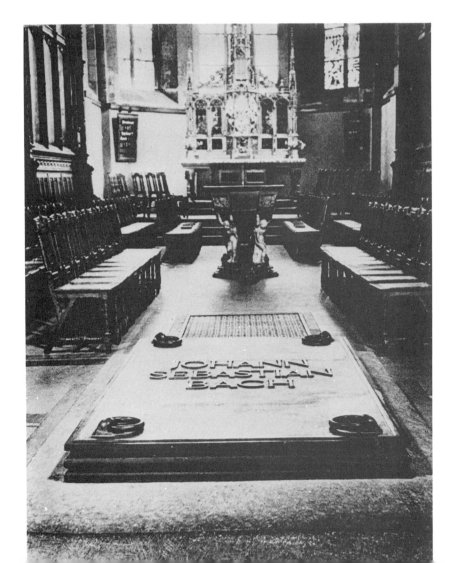

Bach's present tomb in the Thomaskirche

Johann Sebastian Bach

List of Musical Works

LITURGICAL
Christmas Oratorio (6 cantatas), 1734
Easter Oratorio, 1736
Kyrie and Gloria, F ma
Kyrie and Gloria, G mi
Kyrie and Gloria, A ma
Kyrie and Gloria, G ma
Magnificant, D ma
Mass in B mi, 1733-8

MOTETS
   Der Geist hilft unserer Schwachheit auf, 1729
   Fürchte dich nicht, 1726
   Jesu, meine Freude, 1723
   Komm, Jesu, komm
Passion according to St John, 1723
Passion according to St Matthew, 1729

PSALMS
   No 117; Lobet den Herrn, alle Heiden
   No 149, Singet dem Herrn ein neues Lied

SANCTUS
   D ma
   C ma
   D ma
   D mi
   G ma

CHURCH CANTATAS
Ach Gott, vom Himmel sieh darein; No 2, c. 1740
Ach Gott, wie manches Herzeleid; No 3, 1740
Ach Gott, wie manches Herzeleid; No 58, 1733

Ach Herr, mich armen Sünder; No 135, c. 1740

Ach, ich sehe itzt; No 162, 1715

Ach lieben Christen, seid getrost; No 114, c. 1740

Ach wie flüchtig, ach wie nichtig; No 26, c. 1740

Allein zu dir, Herr Jesu Christ; No 33, c. 1740

Alles nur nach Gottes Willen; No 72, c. 1726

Also hat Gott die Welt geliebt; No 68, ?1735

Am Abend aber desselbigen Sabbats; No 42, 1731

Ärg're dich, o Seele, nicht; No 186, 1723

Auf Christ Himmelfahrt allein; No 128, ?1735

Aus der Tiefe rufe ich, Herr, zu dir; No 131, 1707

Aus tiefer Not schrei ich zu dir; No 38, c. 1740

Barmherziges Herze der ewigen Liebe; No 185, 1715

Bereitet die Wege; No 132, 1715

Bisher habt ihr nichts gebeten in meinem Namen; No 87, ?1735

Bleib' bei uns, denn es will Abend werden; No 6; 1736

Brich dem Hungrigen dein Brot; No 39, c. 1725

Bringet dem Herrn Ehre; No 148, c. 1725

Christ lag in Todesbanden; No 4, 1724

Christ unser Herr zum Jordan kam; No 7, c. 1740

Christen, ätzet diesen Tag; No 63, c. 1723

Christum wir sollen loben schon; No 121, c. 1740

Christus, der ist mein Leben; No 95, ?1732

Das ist je gewisslich wahr; No 141, c. 1721

Das neugebor'ne Kindelein; No 122, ?1742

Dazu ist erschienen der Sohn Gottes; No 40, ?1723

Dem Gerechten muss das Licht; No 195, ?1726

Denn du wirst meine Seele nicht in der Hölle lassen; No 15,
   1704

Der Friede sei mit dir; No 158, c. 1708

Der Herr denket an uns; No 196, 1708

Der Herr ist mein getreuer Hirt; No 112, 1731

Der Himmel lacht, die Erde jubiliret; No 31, 1715

Die Elenden sollen essen; No 75, 1723

Die Himmel erzählen die Ehre Gottes; No 76, 1723

Du Friedfürst, Herr Jesu Christ; No 116, 1744

Du Hirte Israel, höre; No 104, c. 1725

Du sollst Gott, deinem Herrn, lieben; No 77, c. 1725

Du wahrer Gott und Davids Sohn; No 23, 1724

Ehre sei Gott in der Höhe (incomplete); ?1728

Ein feste Burg ist unser Gott; No 80, 1716-30

Ein Herz, das seinen Jesum lebend weiss; No 134, c. 1717-22

Ein ungefärbt Gemüte; No 24, 1723

Er rufet seinen Schafen; No 175, ?1735

Erforsche mich, Gott, und erfahre; No 136, c. 1725

Erfreut euch, ihr Herzen; No 66, 1731

Erfreute Zeit im neuen Bunde; No 83, ?1724
Erhalt uns, Herr, bei deinem Wort; No 126, c. 1740
Erhöhtes Fleisch und Blut; No 173, c. 1718
Erschallet, ihr Lieder; 172, c. 1724
Erwünschtes Freudenlicht; No 184, ?1724
Es erhub sich ein Streit; No 19, 1726
Es ist das Heil uns kommen her; No 9, ?1731
Es ist dir gesagt, Mensch, was gut ist; No 45, c. 1740
Es ist ein trotzig under verwagt Ding; No 176, ?1735
Es ist euch gut, dass ich hingehe; No 108, ?1735
Es ist nichts gesundes an meinem Leibe; No 25, c. 1731
Es reifet euch ein schrecklich Ende; No 90, c. 1740
Es warter Alles auf dich; No 187, 1732
Falsche Welt, dir trau'ich nicht; No 52, c. 1730
Freue dich, erlöste Schaar; No 30, 1738
Geist und Seelle wird verwirret; No 35, ?1731
Gelobet sei der Herr, mein Gott; No 129, 1732
Gelobet seist du, Jesus Christ; No 91, c. 1740
Gleich wie der Regen, und Schnee; No 18, c. 1714
Gloria in excelsis Deo; No 191, c. 1733
Gott, der Herr, ist Sonn' und Schild; No 79, ?1735
Gott fähret auf mit Jauchzen; No 43, 1735
Gott ist mein König; No 71, 1708
Gott ist uns're Zuversicht; No 197
Gott, man lobet dich in der Stille; No 120, 1730
Gott soll allein mein Herze haben; No 169, c. 1731
Gottwie dein Name, so ist dein Ruhm; No 171, ?1730
Gottes Zeit ist die allerbeste Zeit; No 106, ?1707
Gottlob! nun geht das Jahr zu Ende; No 28, c. 1736
Halt' im Gedächtnis Jesum Christ; No 67, c. 1735
Herr Christ, der ein'ge Gottes Sohn; No 96, c. 1740
Herr deine Augen sehen nach dem Glauben; No 102, ?1731
Herr, gehe nicht in's Gericht; No 105, c. 1725
Herr Gott, Beherrscher aller Dinge (incomplete); c. 1740
Herr Gott, dich loben alle wir; No 130, c. 1740
Herr Gott, dich loben wir; No 16, ?1724
Herr Jesu Christ, du höchstes Gut; No 113, c. 1740
Herr Jesu Christ, wahr Mensch und Gott; No 127, c. 1740
Herr, wie du willst, so schick's mit mir; No 73, c. 1725
Herz und Mund und Tat und Leben; No 147, 1716
Himmelskönig, sei willkommen; No 182, 1715
Höchsterwünschtes Freudenfest; No 194, 1723
Ich armer Mensch, ich Sündenknecht; No 55, c. 1731
Ich bin ein guter Hirt; No 85, 1735
Ich bin vergnügt mit meinem Glücke; No 84, 1731
Ich elender Mensch, wer wird mich erlösen; No 48, c. 1740

Ich freue mich in dir; No 133, c. 1735

Ich geh' und suche mit Verlangen; No 49, c. 1731

Ich glaube, lieber Herr, hilf meinem Unglauben; No 109,
c. 1731

Ich habe genug; No 82, c. 1731

Ich hab' in Gottes Herz und Sinn; No 92, c. 1740

Ich habe meine Zuversicht; No 188, c. 1730

Ich hatte viel Bekümmernis; No 21, 1714

Ich lasse dich nicht, du segnest mich denn; No 157, 1727

Ich liebe den Höchsten von ganzem Gemüte; No 174, c. 1731

Ich ruf' zu dir, Herr Jesu Christ; No 177, 1732

Ich steh' mit einem Fuss im Grabe; No 156, ?1730

Ich weiss, dass mein Erlöser lebt; No 160, 1717

Ich will den Kreuzstab gerne tragen; No 56, c. 1731

Ihr, die euch von Christo nennet; No 164, c. 1723

Ihr Menschen, rühmet Gottes Leben; No 167, c. 1725

Ihr Pforten zu Zion (incomplete) No 193, c. 1740

Ihre werdet weinen und heulen; No 103, c. 1735

In allen meinem Taten; No 97, 1734

Jauchzeit Gott in allen Landen; No 51, c. 1731

Jesu, der du meine Seele; No 78, c. 1740

Jesu, nun sei gepreiset; No 41, ?1736

Jesus nahm zu die Zwölfe; No 22, 1723

Jesus schläft, was soll ich hoffen?; No 81, 1724

Komm, du süsse Todesstunde; No 161, 1715

Leichtgesinnte Flattergeister; No 181, c. 1725

Liebster Gott, wann werd' ich sterben?; No 8, c. 1725

Liebster Immanuel, Herzog der Frommen; No 123, c. 1740

Liebster Jesu, mein Verlangen; No 32, c. 1740

Lobe den Herrn, den mächtigen König der Ehren; No 137,
?1732

Lobe den Herrn, meine Seele; No 69, ?1724

Lobe den Herrn, meine Seele; No 143, 1735

Lobet Gott in seinen Reichen; No 11, c. 1735

Mache dich, mein Geist bereit; No 115, c. 1740

Man singet mit Freuden vom Sieg; No 149, 1731

Mein Gott, wie lang', ach lange; No 155, 1716

Mein Herze schwimmt im Blut; c. 1714

Mein liebster Jesu ist verloren; No 154, 1724

Meine Seel'erhebt den Herrn; No 10, c. 1740

Meine Seele, rühmt und preist; No 189, c. 1707

Meine Seufzer, meine Tränen; No 13, c. 1736

Meinen Jesum lass' ich nicht; No 124, c. 1740

Mit Fried' und Freud' ich fahr' dahin; No 125, c. 1740

Nach dir, Herr, verlanget mich; No 150, c. 1710

Nimm von uns, Herr, du treuer Gott; No 101, c. 1740

Nimm was dein ist, und gehe hin; No 144, c. 1725
Nun danket alle Gott; No 192, ?1732
Nun ist das Heil und die Kraft; No 50, c. 1749
Nun komm, der Heiden Heiland; No 61, 1714
Nun komm, der Heiden Heiland; No 62, c. 1740
Nur Jedem das Seine; No 163, 1715
O ewiges Feuer; (incomplete) c. 1730
O ewiges Feuer; No 34, c. 1740
O Ewigkeit, du Donnerwort; No 20, c. 1725
O Ewigkeit, du Donnerwort; No 60, 1732
O heil'ges Geist und Wasserbad; No 165, ?1724
O Jesu Christ, mein's Lebens Licht; No 118, c. 1737
Preise, Jerusalem, den Herrn; No 119, 1723
Schau, lieber Gott, wie meine Feind; No 153, 1724
Schauet und sehet; No 46, c. 1725
Schalge doch, gewünschte Stunde; No 53, 1723-34
Schmücke dich, o liebe Seele; No 180, c. 1740
Schwingt freudig euch empor; No 36, c. 1730
Sehet welch' eine Liebe; No 64, ?1723
Sehet, wir geh'n hinauf den Jerusalem; No 159, ?1729
Sei Lob und Ehr' dem höchsten Gut; No 117, c. 1733
Selig ist der Mann; No 57, c. 1740
Sie werden aus Saba alle kommen; No 65, 1724
Sie werden euch in den Bann tun; No 44, c. 1725
Sie werden euch in den Bann tun; No 183, c. 1735
Siehe ich will viel Fischer aussenden; No 88, 1732
Siehe zu, dass deine Gottesfurcht nicht Heuchelei sei; No 179,
    ?1724
Singet dem Herrn ein neues Lied; No 190, c. 1725
So du mit deinem Munde bekennest Jesum; No 145, c. 1729
Süsser Trost, mein Jesus kommt; No 151, c. 1740
Tritt auf die Glaubensbahn; No 152, c. 1715
Tue Rechnung Donnerwort; No 168, c. 1725
Uns ist ein Kind geboren; No 142, c. 1714
Unser Mund sei voll Lachens; No 110
Vernügte Ruh', beliebte Seelenlust; No 170, ?1732
Wachet auf, ruft uns die Stimme; No 140, c. 1731
Wachet, betet, seid bereit allezeit; No 70, 1716
Wahrlich, ich sage euch; No 86, c. 1725
War' Gott nicht mit uns diese Zeit; No 14, 1735
Warum betrübst du dich, mein Herz; No 138, c. 1740
Was frag' ich nach der Welt; No 94, ?1734
Was Gott tut, das ist wohlgetan; No 98, c. 1732
Was Gott tut, das ist wohlgetan; No 99, c. 1734
Was Gott tut, das ist wohlgetan; No 100, ?1735
Was mein Gott will, das g'scheh' allzeit; No 111, c. 1740

Was soll ich aus dir machen; No 89, c. 1730

Was willst du dich betrüben; No 107, ?1735

Weinen, Klagen, Sorgen, Zagen; No 12, c. 1724

Wer da glaubet und getauft wird; No 37, c. 1727

Wer Dank opfert, der preiset mich; No 17, c. 1737

Wer mich liebet, der wird mein Wort halten; No 59, 1716

Wer mich liebet, der wird mein Work halten; No 74, ?1735

Wer nur den lieben Gott lässt walten; No 93, ?1728

Wer sich selbst erhöhet, der soll erniedriget werden; No 47,
    ?1720

Wer weiss wie nahe mir mein Ende; No 27, 1731

Widerstehe doch der Stünde; No 54, 1723-34

Wie schön leuchtet der Morgenstern; No 1, c. 1740

Wir danken dir, Gott, wir danken dir; No 29, 1731

Wir müssen durch viel Trübsal; No 146, c. 1740

Wo gehest du hin?; No 166, c. 1725

Wo Gott der Herr nicht bei uns halt; No 178, c. 1740

Wo soll ich fliehen hin?; No 55, 1735

Wohl dem, der sich auf seinen Gott; No 139, c. 1740

SECULAR CANTATAS

Amore traditore

Angenehmes Wiederau, 1737

Auf, schmetternde Töne; 1734

Coffee Cantata; 1732

Durchlaucht'ster Leopold; ?1718

Freude reget sich, Die; 1726

Ich bin in mir vernügt; c. 1730

Mit Gnaden bekröne der Himmel die Zeiten; ?1721

Non sa che sia dolore

O angenehme Melodei; ?1747

O holder Tag

Peasant Cantata; 1742

Preise dein Glücke; 1734

Schleicht, spielende Wellen; 1734

Schwingt freudig euch empor; 1726

Streit zwischen Phoebus und Pan; ?1731

Tönet, ihr Pauken!

Trauer Ode, 1727

Vereinigte Zwietracht der wechsenden Saiten, 1726

Vergnügte Pleissen-Stadt; 1728

Wahl des Herkules; 1733

Was mir behagt, ist nur die muntre Jagd; 1716

Weichet nur, betrübte Schatten; c. 1720

Zufriedensgestellte Aeolus, Der; 1725

Manuscript of the aria "Christi Gleider, ach bedenket"

Manuscript page from the D-major harpsichord concerto

ORCHESTRAL WORKS
Brandenburg Concertos
  1 F ma
  2 F ma
  3 G ma
  4 G ma
  5 D ma
  6 Bb ma
Overtures (Suites)
  1 C ma
  2 B mi
  3 D ma
  4 D ma
Sinfonia in D ma (incomplete)

CONCERTOS
Violin, A mi
Violin, E ma
2 Violins, D mi
Clavier, A ma
Clavier, D ma
Clavier, D mi
Clavier, E ma
Clavier, F ma
Clavier, F mi
Clavier, G mi
2 Claviers, C ma
2 Claviers, C mi
2 Claviers, C mi
3 Claviers, C ma
3 Claviers, D mi
4 Claviers, A mi
Clavier, flute, violin; A mi

CHAMBER MUSIC
6 Sonatas (partitas) for violin
  1 G mi
  2 A mi
  3 C ma
  4 B mi
  5 D mi
  6 E ma
6 Suites (Sonatas) for cello
  1 G ma
  2 D mi
  3 C ma

4 Eb ma

5 C mi

6 D ma

ONE INSTRUMENT WITH CONTINUO
Fugue for violin, G mi
Sonata for violin, E mi
Sonata for violin, G ma
3 Sonatas for flute

1 C ma

2 E mi

3 E ma

TWO INSTRUMENTS WITH CONTINUO
Canon for flute and violin, C mi
The Musical Offering
Sonata for 2 violins, C ma
Sonata for flute and violin, C mi
Sonata for flute and violin, G ma
Sonata for 2 flutes, G ma

CLAVIER AND ONE INSTRUMENT
3 Sonatas for clavier and flute

1 B mi

2 Eb ma

3 A mi

3 Sonatas for clavier and viola da gamba

1 G ma

2 D ma

3 G mi

6 Sonatas for clavier and violin

1 B mi

2 A ma

3 E ma

4 C mi

5 F mi

6 G ma

Suite in A ma for clavier and violin

ORGAN WORKS
Alla breve pro organo pleno D ma
Aria, F ma
Canzona, D mi
Choral Preludes

Catechism Preludes – Clavierübung, Vol III
Eighteen Preludes
Komm, heiliger Geist, Herre Gott
Komm, heiliger Geist, Herre Gott
An Wasserflüssen Babylon
Schmücke dich, O liebe Seele
Herr Jesu Christ, dich zu uns wend
O Lamm Gottes unschuldig
Nun danket alle Gott
Von Gott will ich nicht lassen
Nun komm der Heiden Heiland (3 versions)
Allein Gott in der Hoh' sei Ehr (3 versions)
Jesus Christus, unser Heiland (2 versions)
Komm Gott, Schöpfer, heiliger Geist
Vor deinen Tron tret' ich
Kirnberger's Collection
Wer nur den lieben Gott lässt walten (2 versions)
Ach Gott und Herr (2 versions)
Wo soll ich fliehen hin
Christ lag in Todesbanden
Christum wir wollen loben schon
Gelobet seist du, Jesu Christ
Herr Christ, der ein'ge Gottes-Sohn
Nun komm der Heiden Heiland
Vom Himmel hoch da komm' ich her (2 versions)
Das Jesulein soll doch mein Trost
Gottes Sohn ist kommen
Lob sei dem allmächtigen Gott
Durch Adams Fall ist ganz verderbt
Liebster Jesu wir sind hier (2 versions)
Ich hab' mein' Sach' Gott heinsgesetellt (2 versions)
Herr Jesu Christ dich zu uns wend'
Wir Christenleut'
Allein Gott in der Hoh' sei Ehr'
In dich hab' ich gehoffet, Herr
Jesu, meine Freude
Miscellaneous Preludes
Ach Gott und Herr
Allein Gott in der Höh' sei Ehr' (3 versions)
An Wasserflüssen Babylon
Christ lag in Todesbanden
Der Tag der ist so freudenreich
Ein' fest Burg ist unser Gott
Erbarm' dich mein, O Herre Gott
Gelobet seist du, Jesu Christ (2 versions)
Gottes Sohn ist kommen

Herr Gott, dich loben wir
Herr Jesu Christ, dich zu uns wend
Herzlich tut mich verlangen
Jesus, meine Zuversicht
In dulci jubilo
Liebster Jesu, wir sind hier (2 versions)
Lobt Gott, ihr Christen allzugleich
Meine Seele erhebt den Herren
Nun freut euch, lieben Christen g'mein
Valet will ich dir geben (2 versions)
Vater unser im Himmelreich
Vom Himmel hoch da komm' ich her
Wie schön leuchtet der Morgenstern
Wir glauben all' an einen Gott

Orgelbüchlein

Nun komm der Heiden Heiland
Gott durch deine Güte
Herr Christ, der ein'ge Gottes-Sohn
Lob sei dem allmächtigen Gott
Puer natus in Bethlehem
Gelobet seist du, Jesu Christ
Der Tag, der ist so freudenreich
Vom Himmel hoch da komm' ich her
Vom Himmel kam der Engel Schaar
In dulci jubilo
Lobt Gott, ihr Christen, allzugleich
Jesu, meine Freude
Christum wir sollen loben schon
Wir Christenleut
Helft mir Gottes Güte preisen
Das alte Jahr vergangen ist
In dir ist Freude
Mit Fried' und Freud' ich fahr' dahin
Herr Gott, nun schleuss den Himmel auf
O Lamm Gottes, unschuldig
Christe, du Lamm Gottes
Christus, der uns selig macht
Da Jesus an dem Kreuze stund
O Mensch, bewein' dein' Sünde gross
Wir danken dir, Herr Jesu Christ
Hilf Gott, dass mir's gelinge
Christ lag in Todesbanden
Jesus Christus, unser Heiland
Christ ist erstanden
Erstanden ist der heil'ge Christ
Erschienen ist der herrlich' Tag

Heut' triumphiret Gottes Sohn
Komm, Gott, Schöpfer, heiliger Geist
Herr Jesu Christ, dich zu uns wend
Liebster Jesu, wir sind hier (2 versions)
Dies sind die heil'gen zehn Gebo
Vater unser im Himmelreich
Durch Adams Fall ist ganz verderbt
Er ist das Heil uns kommen her
Ich ruf' zu dir, Herr Jesu Christ
In dich hab' ich gehoffet, Herr
Wenn wir in höchsten Nöten sein
Wer nur den lieben Gott lässt walten
Alle Menschen mussen sterben
Ach wie nichtig, ach wie flüchtig

Schübler's Book

Wachet auf, ruft uns die Stimme
Wo soll ich fliehen hin
Wer nur den lieben Gott lässt walten
Meine Seele erhebt den Herren
Ach bleib' bei uns, Herr Jesu Christ
Kommst du nun, Jesu, vom Himmel herunter

4 Concertos, A mi, 2 C ma, G ma
4 Duets
5 Fantasies
2 Fantasies and Fugues
Fantasy C mi
Fantasy C ma (incomplete)
Fantasy and Fugue, A mi
Fugue, C mi (incomplete)
3 Fugues, C mi, D ma, G ma
4 Fugues, B mi, C mi, G ma, G mi
Kleines harmonisches Labyrinth
Passacaglia, C mi
Pastorale, F ma
Pedal Exercise, G mi
4 Preludes
4 Preludes and Fugues
9 Preludes and Fugues
5 Preludes and Fugues
8 Short Preludes and Fugues
6 Sonatas
Toccata and Fugue, E ma
4 Toccatas and Fugues
3 Trios
4 Variations on Chorales (Partitas)
Fugue in D mi, arranged for organ

139

CLAVIER WORKS

Aria Variata, A mi,
Goldberg Variations, 1742
Capriccio in honorem J C Bach
Capricio sopra la lontananza del suo fratello
Chromatic Fantasy and Fugue
Clavierbüchlein vor Anna Magdalena Bach
Clavierbüchlein vor Wilhelm Friedemann Bach
Concerto in the Italian Style, F ma
Duet for 2 Claviers, F ma
4 Duets
Fantasy, C mi
Fantasy, G mi
Fantasy, C mi
Fantasy, A mi
Fantasy, C mi
Fantasy and Fugue, A mi
Fantasy and Fugue, A mi
Fughetta, C mi
Fugue, C mi (unfinished)
5 Fugues, C ma, C mi, 2 D mi, E mi
5 Fugues, 3 A ma, A mi, B mi
12 Little Preludes
Partita B mi
6 Partitas
Prelude, A mi
Prelude, E mi (unfinished)
2 Preludes A mi, C mi
4 Preludes and Fughettas D mi, E mi, F ma, G ma
Prelude and Fugue, A mi
Prelude and Fugue A mi
Prelude and Fugue, Eb ma
6 Preludes for Beginners
Sonata, A mi
Sonata, D ma
Suite, A mi
Suite, D mi
Suite, Eb ma
Suite, F ma
2 Suites, A ma, F mi
2 Suites, Bb ma, C mi
6 Suites ('English')
6 Suites ('French')
5 Toccatas
2 Toccatas
Das Wohltemperierte Clavier, Books I and II

Manuscript page from the *Clavierbüchlein vor W.F. Bach*

Manuscript page from one of the solo violin sonatas

Final words from many of his manuscripts: "Fine. Soli Deo Gloria."

ARRANGEMENTS FOR CLAVIER
Adagio, G ma
16 Concertos
Fugue, Bb ma
Fugue, Bb ma
Sonata, D mi
2 Sonatas, A mi, C ma
Suite from the third Partita, E ma

VOICE AND CLAVIER
5 Songs from Anna Magdalena's Notenbuch

FOUR VOICES AND CONTINUO
Quodlibet

UNSPECIFIED MEDIUM
The Art of the Fugue

ILLUSTRATIONS ADDED FOR THE EXPANDED EDITION

In creating this expanded edition, more than fifty illustrations have been added as un-numbered pages within the text. Following is a key to those insertions.

facing page

Monument to Bach 6
Johann Ambrosius Bach 7
Bach Family tree 7
Georgenkirche organ 8
Michaeliskirche 9
Bach's school 9
Palace of Celle 24
J.A. Reinken 24
J.S. Bach 25
Neue Kirche, Arnstadt 25
Blasiuskirche organ 38
J.A. Frohne 39
G.C. Eilmar 39
Cantata Manuscript 40
Duke of Saxe-Weimar 41
Prince of Saxe-Weimar 42
Wilhelmsburg Palace 42
Schlosskirche, Weimar 43
Louis Marchand 52
Manuscript of *Orgelbuchlein* 52
Leopold of Cothen 53
Bach in 1720 62
Brandenburg concerto manuscript 62
Margrave of Brandenburg 63
Castle of Cothen 63
Frederica of Cothen 66
Title page of "Well-Tempered Clavier" 67
J.H. Ernesti 72
Contract with Leipzig 72
Title page of *Clavierbuchlein* 73
Johann Kuhnau 73
Bach's organ in Leipzig 78
Title page of *Christmas Oratorio* 79
Text page of *Christmas Oratorio* 79
Manuscript of *St. Matthew Passion* 88
Display of instruments 89
Title page of *Clavier-Ubung I* 89
Page from the *Coffee Cantata* 94
J.S. Bach 95
Manuscript of canon 95
Frauenkirche organ 102
Sophienkirche organ 102
J.S. Bach 103
Page from the *Musical Offering* 103
Page from "Well-Tempered Clavier" 112
Bust of Bach 113
Page of chorale prelude 113
J.S. Bach 120
Page from *The Art of the Fugue* 120
Petition of his widow 121
Her signature 121
Bach's sarcophagus 128
Tomb in the Thomaskirche 128
Bust of Bach 129
Manuscript of aria 134
Page of harpsichord concerto 135
Page from notebook for his son 140
Page from solo violin sonata 141
Conclusion of manuscripts 141

Index

Ahle, JG 33, 35, 38
Arnstadt 8, 25, 27-32, 40
Art of the Fugue 115, 119
Augustus, Elector of Saxony 80

B Minor Mass 98, 113
Bach, Anna Magdalena 63, 66, 111,
   112, 120
Bach, CPE 42, 57, 72, 103, 106, 111,
   114, 120-1
Bach, Catherina Dorothea 42, 72
Bach, Christoph 8
Bach, Gottfried Bernhard 72
Bach, Heinrich 8
Bach, Johannes 8
Bach, Johann Ambrosius 7-10
Bach, Johann Bernhard 50, 103
Bach, Johann Christian 103, 110, 120
Bach, Johann Christoph 9, 10, 17, 19
Bach, Johann Elias, 109, 111, 112
Bach, Johann Jakob, 10, 17, 32
Bach, Johann Lorenz, 50
Bach, Johann Michael 27
Bach, Maria Barbara 27, 31-2, 35, 42,
   59
Bach, Vitus 8
Bach, Wilhelm Friedemann 42, 56,
   72, 99, 100
Baroque 39-40
Beethoven, Ludwig van 125
Berlin 114
Böhm, Georg 23
Brandenburg Concertos 54, 60-2
Buxtehude, Dietrich 29-30, 35

Carlsbad 59-60
Celle 24
Christmas Oratorio 79, 98
Coffee Cantata 96
Collegium Musicum 96, 105
Cöthen 51-66, 71

Doctrine of Affections 78
Dornheim 34-5
Dresden 51, 95, 100, 107, 119
Drese, JS 51
Drese, JW 46, 51

Effler, Johann 27, 39
Eilmar, GC 38
Eisenach, 7-11, 17, 25
Erdmann, Georg 20, 91
Erfurt 8, 12
Ernesti, JA 103-5
Ernesti, JH 72, 90
Ernst, Johann 29

Franck, Salomo 43
Frederick Augustus I, Elector of
   Saxony 84-5, 97-8
Frederick the Great 114-7
Frohne, JA 38-9

Gegenbach 29
Gerhardt, Paul 37, 66
Gesner, JM 90-5, 103
Gleitsmann, Paul 27
Goldberg Variations 102, 113-4
Görner, JG 80-1
Göttingen 94, 103
Graupner, Christoph 69, 71

Halle 7, 43-6, 56, 108
Hamburg 21-4, 59-60, 67, 69
Handel, George Frederick 7, 54-5
Harrer, Gottlob 119-20
Henrici, CF 79-86
Herd, Johann Balthasar 22
Herda, Elias 19

Italian Concerto 102

Kirchbach, HC von 81
Kobelius, JA 25
Koch, JG 7
Krebs, JT 50
Kuhnau, Johann 44, 67

Lämmerhirt, Elizabeth 9-10
Lämmerhirt, Tobias 35
Leibnitz, Gottfried von 12-14
Leipzig 67- passim
Leopold, Prince of Anhalt Cöthen
  51-4, 59, 66-72
Little Clavier Book 56-8, 63
Little Organ Book 50
Louis XIV 11, 13
Lübeck 22, 24, 29
Lübeck, Vincenz 24
Ludewig, BD 83-4
Lüneberg 19-24, 90
Luther, Martin 8, 48
Lutheranism, 11-2, 17, 54

Magnificat 79
Marchand, Louis 51
Mendelssohn, Felix 124-5
Mozart, LA 125
Mühlhausen 33, 35, 38-41, 103
Musical Offering, The 102, 115, 119

Ohrdruf 10, 17, 19, 22

Pachelbel, Johann 10
Peasant Cantata 98
Picander 79, 86, 96
Pietism 38, 78
Potsdam 115, 120
Praetorius, FE 21

Reinken, JA 23-4
Rolle, CF 44

Sachsen-Weissenfels, Duke of 25
St Blaise's, Mühlhausen 33, 35-6
St Boniface, Arnstadt 25, 31
St Catherine's, Hamburg 23
St George's, Eisenach 9-10, 37
St James', Hamburg 60
St John's, Lüneberg 23
St Mary's, Lübeck 29-30
St Mary's, Mülhausen 35, 38, 104
St Michael's, Lüneberg 19, 21-4
St Nicholas', Leipzig 75-6, 84, 94, 98
St Paul's, Leipzig 80-2
St Sophia's, Dresden 100
St Thomas', Leipzig 69 passim
St John Passion 69, 75-8, 87
St Matthew Passion, 72, 86, 125
Salle, de la 24
Sangerhausen 25
Saxe-Weimar, Duke of 39
Scheibe, JA 107-9
Schubart, JM 35, 50
Schweinfurth, 112, 115
Stauber, JL 35

Taylor, Chevalier John 120
Telemann, GP 67, 96
Trebs, Heinrich 42

Vivaldi, Antonio 47-8, 61

Wartburg 8-9
Wecker, CG 82-3
Weigel, Christoph 102
Weimar, 39, 41-9, 90
Well-Tempered Clavier, The 62
Wesley, SS 125
Wilhelm Ernst, Duke of Saxe-Weimar
  41-3

Zschortau 113

780.92 Bac
Dowley, Tim.
Bach, his life and times

780.92 Bac
Dowley, Tim.
Bach, his life and times

HOWELL CARNEGIE LIBRARY,
HOWELL, MICHIGAN 48843